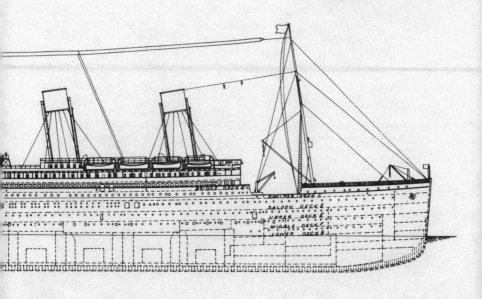

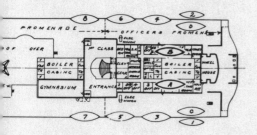

BOAT DECK.

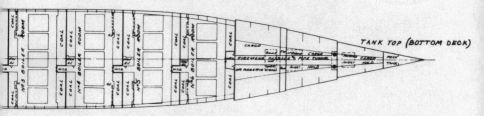

TANK TOP (BOTTOM DECK)

THE NIGHT LIVES ON

ALSO BY WALTER LORD

The Miracle of Dunkirk
Lonely Vigil
The Dawn's Early Light
Incredible Victory
The Past That Would Not Die
Peary to the Pole
A Time to Stand
The Good Years
Day of Infamy
A Night to Remember
The Fremantle Diary

THE NIGHT LIVES ON

BY

WALTER LORD

WILLIAM MORROW AND COMPANY, INC.

NEW YORK

Library of Congress Cataloging-in-Publication Data

Lord, Walter, 1917–
  The night lives on.

  Includes index.
  1. Titanic (steamship)   I. Title.
G530.T6L56   1986   910'.091631   86-5182
ISBN 0-688-04939-7

Printed in the United States of America

First Edition

1 2 3 4 5 6 7 8 9 10

FOR

J. FRANK SUPPLEE IV

Contents

THE NIGHT LIVES ON

CHAPTER I

Unsinkable Subject

Just 20 minutes short of midnight, April 14, 1912, the great new White Star Liner *Titanic,* making her maiden voyage from Southampton to New York, had a rendezvous with ice in the calm, dark waters of the North Atlantic. She brushed the berg so gently that many on board didn't notice it, but so lethally that she was instantly doomed.

By midnight Captain Edward J. Smith knew the worst, and ordered the lifeboats filled and lowered. There were distressingly few of these, enough for only a third of the ship's company. The rule was, of course, "Women and children first." At 12:15 A.M. the *Titanic* sent her first distress call. At 12:45 she began firing rockets, for there was a light on the horizon, tantalizingly near. The light remained motionless.

On the *Titanic,* the ship's bellboys—lads of 14 or 15— brought up loaves of bread for the lifeboats, now dropping one after another into the sea. Far below, the engineers kept the lights burning; topside, the band played

cheerful music on the Boat Deck. The ship was notice-
ably down at the bow.

At 1:10, as Boat 1 pulled away, the water lapped the
portholes just under the ship's name. Thirty minutes
later, as Collapsible C rowed off, the name had vanished
into the sea, and the forward well deck was awash. The
lights still burned, and the band still played.

By 2:05 the last boat had been launched, leaving 1,600
people stranded on the sloping decks. Richard N.
Williams II, a 19-year-old First Class passenger, wan-
dered into the main companionway on A Deck and idly
watched the water creeping up the grand staircase. On
the paneled wall nearby hung a handsomely framed
chart, pins still in place, marking the *Titanic*'s daily
progress across the Atlantic. The lights still burned, now
with a reddish glow. The band probably played on, but
no one is sure.

At 2:17 the *Titanic* slowly, almost majestically, stood
on end. The lights blinked once and went out forever.
Then came a thundering roar, as everything movable
within the ship broke loose and plunged downward.
The great hull itself sagged as though finally defeated.
At 2:20 she settled back slightly and slipped beneath the
sea. Over 1,500 people were lost in this, the greatest
maritime disaster in history.

Understandably, the sinking of the *Titanic* was a sen-
sation at the time. The morning after the rescue ship
Carpathia reached New York with her pitiful load of 705
survivors, *The New York Times* devoted its first 12 pages
to the story. But a single letter in the Manuscript Division of the Library of Congress gives a more vivid picture of the universal shock and grief than any number

of newspaper pages. The letter is from a young naval officer, Alexander Macomb, to his mother. It is dated April 16, 1912, and describes what happened as he emerged from a pleasant evening at the theater. . . .

> The terrible news about the *Titanic* reached New York about 11 o'clock last night, and the scene on Broadway was awful. Crowds of people were coming out of the theaters, cafes were going full tilt, when the newsboys began to cry, "Extra! Extra! *Titanic* sunk with 1800 aboard!" You can't imagine the effect of those words on the crowd. Nobody could realize what had happened, and when they did begin to understand, the excitement was almost enough to cause a panic in the theaters. Women began to faint and weep, and scores of people in evening clothes jumped into cabs and taxis and rushed to the offices of the White Star Line, where they remained all night waiting for news. . . .

Understandable then, but there have been massive changes in the world since 1912. We don't even cross the ocean the same way now, and two great wars have numbed us to casualty lists. Compared to the implications of a nuclear confrontation, the figures of "souls lost" in a shipwreck—any shipwreck—seem almost quaint. Given the world today, one might suppose that people would no longer be gripped by the *Titanic*. Not so. She has never been more with us than now.

The discovery of her hulk in September 1985 created a wave of excitement that seemed in sharp contrast to the silent gray ghost resting so peacefully on the ocean floor. My own connection with the *Titanic* is peripheral at best—and with the expedition that found her, it is nil—yet no less than 32 requests for interviews poured in from radio, television, and the press over the next ten days.

There seems no limit to the public's fascination. In America every survivor now rates an obituary in *The New York Times.* Typical was the case of 90-year-old Ethel Beane, who died in Rochester, New York, in 1983. She had lived a blameless but utterly uneventful life. She hadn't even told her *Titanic* experiences for 71 years. But she was nevertheless newsworthy—simply by being a survivor.

No story is too farfetched, as long as it bears the magic label "Titanic." In London *The Times* recently reported that a Los Angeles businessman planned to build three replicas of the *Titanic* for $1.5 *billion.* Each would accommodate 600 passengers at $1,000 a day. Preposterous? Nevertheless, *The Times* featured the story on the front page. The editor knew that the *Titanic* is always news.

Over the years the ship has become an enduring favorite on stage and screen. She has been the locale for five major motion pictures and played an important part in many others. In 1976 she was the setting for an off-Broadway production. In 1980 she was the subject of an opera jointly produced by the Berlin Opera and the UCLA Fine Arts Productions. In 1983 she was "raised" from the Thames in an extravaganza at the London International Festival of Theatre.

Meanwhile on television she played a crucial role in *Upstairs, Downstairs,* the memorable series about the Bellamy family. Going down with the ship, "Lady

Marjorie Bellamy" joined "Edward" and "Edith" of Noel Coward's *Cavalcade* as probably the most famous of all the fictional victims of the disaster.

Gradually the *Titanic* has ceased to be merely a shipwreck; she has become a symbol. In Hitler's Germany, Joseph Goebbels used her to portray English decadence and cowardice. In postwar Germany, the message was different, but the *Titanic* was still a symbol. This time the producers were drawing a parallel between the disaster and the decision to deploy Pershing missiles on German soil. Both were seen as examples of technology out of control. A single miscalculation—a momentary lapse in judgment—could bring appalling destruction.

Not surprisingly, the *Titanic* has also become a great favorite with political cartoonists. She is completely nonpartisan: since 1976 she has been used to depict the troubles of Presidents Ford, Carter, and Reagan. In British cartoons both the ship and the iceberg have represented Prime Minister Margaret Thatcher. The lost liner, poised for her final plunge, even graced the cover of *Punch* in April 1975 as "England's Glory."

This continuing fascination has seen a boom in the price of *Titanic* memorabilia. Contemporary books and pamphlets costing less than a dollar in the 1950's now routinely go for $45–$50. Recently a 1912 printed list of the *Titanic*'s passengers—with handwritten notations on where they lived and what happened to them—was sold at auction for $5,000, although no one seemed to know who drew up the list or why.

With the supply of original items running low, a lively industry has sprung up turning out new artifacts. Novelty stores do a brisk business selling *"Titanic"* belt buckles, key chains, and T-shirts. A prominent New York charity has been using replicas of the ship's stationery as a direct-mail eye-catcher. There are even *"Titanic"* bumper stickers, put out by the *Titanic* Historical Society, which does a far greater service by reprinting rare publications that are of immense value to the serious student.

What is the hold of this long-lost liner? Why are people still so fascinated by her? First of all, the *Titanic* must surely be the greatest news story of modern times: the biggest ship in the world, proclaimed unsinkable, hits an iceberg on her maiden voyage and goes down, taking with her many of the best-known celebrities of the day.

Add to that glamour all those "if only's"—if only she had paid more attention to the warnings she received . . . if only the last warning had even reached the bridge . . . if only the wireless operator hadn't cut off one final attempt to reach her . . . if only she had sighted the ice a few seconds sooner, or a few seconds later . . . if only there had been enough lifeboats . . . if only the watertight bulkheads had gone one deck higher . . . if only that ship on the horizon had come . . . if only, if only.

The story has something for everyone. For nautical enthusiasts, it is the ultimate shipwreck. For moralists, there are all those sermons on overconfidence and self-sacrifice. For mystics, the omens are irresistible, from Morgan Robertson's prophetic novel *Futility* of 1898 to presidential aide Archie Butt's strangely foreboding letter assuring his sister-in-law, "If the old ship goes down, you'll find my affairs in shipshape condition."

The *Titanic* is also a trivia lover's dream. What was the name of John Jacob Astor's dog? (Kitty) Who led the band? (Wallace Hartley) Which smokestack was the dummy? (The fourth)

Above all, the *Titanic* entrances the social historian. She is such an exquisite microcosm of the Edwardian world, illuminating so perfectly the class distinctions that prevailed at the time. These distinctions remained sacred even as the ship was going down. One prominent passenger later complained that more First Class men might have been saved, if only steerage passengers hadn't taken up so much room in what he called "the First Class boats." It never occurred to him that the lifeboats, wherever located, might have been for everyone.

There were all too few boats anyhow, leading to a clash between two basic Edwardian rules of conduct. Should normal Class Precedence prevail, or the rule of "Women and children first"? The latter won out officially, but there were cases of both that night.

After the disaster there was a good deal of pondering about all this. Finally, the prestigious *Nautical Magazine* came up with the daring proposition that there should be boats for all, whatever their class. The same applied to wireless, even on ships engaged in the emigrant and coolie trades. "Even coolies are human," the editors explained, "and as such are burdened with souls, also family ties, etc."

The *Titanic* also gives a fascinating picture of post-Edwardian life at its more rarefied level. The damage claim filed by Mrs. Charlotte Cardeza of Philadelphia lists 14 trunks, 4 suitcases, 3 crates, and a medicine chest. Among other things, they contained 70 dresses, 10 fur coats, 38 large feather pieces, 22 hatpins to keep them in place, 91 pairs of gloves, and innumerable trifles to amuse her, like a Swiss music box in the shape of a bird.

The gentleman traveler was similarly burdened. Billy Carter, another fashionable Philadelphian, lost not only his 35-hp Renault motorcar, but 60 shirts, 15 pairs of shoes, two sets of tails, and 24 polo sticks. Even men of moderate means had a surfeit of luggage. Archie Butt, President Taft's military aide, was on a trip of less than six weeks, yet he still needed seven trunks to carry his wardrobe.

Yet none of this is enough to explain the *Titanic*'s current grip on the public. Her unique attractions were always present in the story, but for over 40 years after the disaster, the ship lay more or less in limbo. From 1913 to 1955, not a single book was published on the subject. Then *A Night to Remember* appeared—it awakened some curiosity, but certainly not enough to account for the *Titanic*'s continuing appeal, which actually seems to be on the rise.

Partly, perhaps, the *Titanic* is the beneficiary of a new interest in all ocean liners. Now that they are gone, people have discovered them. A leisurely voyage seems so much more civilized than being sealed in a tube and shot across the sea.

But more important is the fact that America is currently on a "nostalgia binge." The *Titanic* has come to stand for a world of tranquillity and civility that we have somehow lost. Today life is hectic, prices are climbing, quality is falling, violence is everywhere. In contrast, 1912 looks awfully good—a happier world, where a shoulder of lamb cost 16 cents a pound.

In some ways we're kidding ourselves. The shirt that cost only 23 cents in 1912 was often made by a child who got only $3.54 a week. Harold Bride, the Second Wireless Operator on the *Titanic*, made $20 a month. It would have taken all his pay for 18 years to cross the ocean in style.

And *those* days were violent, too. As we busily build barricades around the White House, it's easy to forget that in 1912 former President Theodore Roosevelt was shot and wounded while running for a third term. TR was perhaps the most popular man in America, yet it didn't save him from a would-be assassin.

There was social injustice then, too. To dramatize the struggle for women's suffrage, Emily Davison died by throwing herself in front of the King's horse during the 1913 running of the Derby.

But in one respect this period really was different. People might argue over how to right the world's wrongs, but they were still sure the wrongs could be righted. In 1912 people had confidence. Now nobody is sure of anything, and the more uncertain we become, the more we long for a happier era when we felt we knew the answers. The *Titanic* symbolizes that era, or more poignantly, the end of it. The worse things get today, the more we think of her, and all that went down with her.

Whatever the explanation, there seems no limit to the thirst for fresh information—or to the number of eager researchers who stand ready to supply it. Many have carved out for themselves special niches in the story. A man in Wisconsin thinks that the *Titanic* was "under-ruddered," meaning that the area of her rudder was too small. He has interesting comparison figures with the

Mauretania and other liners. A retired editor in Toronto has become an expert on the ship's watertight and pumping arrangements. He points out that by far the best pumps were in the two engine rooms, where they were never needed—one more ironic twist to the story. A boy in North Carolina is painstakingly putting the passengers in their proper staterooms. A Dutch researcher is fascinated by Fifth Officer Lowe and has been a real Sherlock Holmes in tracking down Lowe's family.

The personalities on the *Titanic* offer an especially fertile field for investigation. A recent biography explores the life of Second Officer Lightoller, whose adventurous career included four shipwrecks and a heroic role at Dunkirk in 1940. A privately published labor of love traces the story of Lolo and Momon Navratil, the so-called *"Titanic* waifs." Their father had kidnapped them from their mother, and was taking them to America under an assumed name to start a new life. He put them in the last lifeboat, stepped back, and went down with the ship. The children were too young to know who they were, and their identity remained a mystery for days.

The subjects range from premonitions before the disaster to the discovery of the *Titanic*'s grave 73 years later. Nothing is overlooked. One recent book even examines the catastrophe from the iceberg's point of view.

One might think that would wind up the subject. Not at all. Scores of riddles remain; these pages explore a few of the most intriguing. . . .

CHAPTER II

What's in a Name?

"**I** name this ship *'Titanic.'*
May God bless her . . . and all who sail in her." The
words are uttered by a regal-looking lady, who then
breaks a bottle of champagne against the bow of the
great ship standing on the stocks. Slowly the vessel slides
down the ways and into the sea, hailed by thousands of
cheering spectators.

It is the opening scene of the film *A Night to Remember*,
and it all seems so natural that one does not question its
authenticity. We scarcely realize that the lady is never
identified. Yet even the script is vague, referring to her
merely as "A Lady."

Who was this lady? Who did christen the *Titanic*? The
answer is: no one. Amazingly enough, the White Star
Line did not go in for the fancy christening ceremony
that usually accompanies the launching of a great liner.
"They just builds 'er and shoves 'er in," explained a
shipyard worker to an inquiring visitor at the time.

Well, not quite. While the ritual of the beribboned

champagne bottle was missing, May 31, 1911, was anything but an ordinary day at Harland & Wolff, the
sprawling Belfast shipyard where the *Titanic* was being
built. The crowds began forming as early as 7:30 A.M.,
when the cross-channel steamer *Duke of Argyll* arrived
from England, loaded with newspapermen and Distinguished Guests. It was, for once, a glorious day—not a
cloud in the sky—and the men's straw hats and the bright
print dresses of the ladies made the occasion seem all
the more festive.

By 11:00 special trams were rolling down Corpora-
tion Street toward the waterfront, packed with local
spectators. The Harbour Commissioners had enclosed a
section of the Albert Quay for those who cared to pay a
few shillings for a good vantage point, and the enclosure
was soon black with people. At 11:15 the railway steamer
Slieve Bearnagh left the Queen's Bridge jetty with another load of paying customers, to join the spectator
fleet already gathering in the River Lagan.

But the men who actually built the *Titanic*—the 14,000
workers of Harland & Wolff—were more inclined to
head for Spencer Basin. Here the grandstands were only
stacks of coal and timber, but the view was good and the
cost was nothing—an important consideration for a
workforce that was paid £2 for a 49-hour week. And
while today was indeed a holiday, it certainly wasn't a
paid holiday, any more than Christmas.

Nobody thought about that just now. Pride was everything. "A Masterpiece of Irish Brains and Industry,"
proclaimed the *Irish News and Belfast Morning News* the
following day. At the moment all eyes were turned on
Slip No. 3, where the *Titanic* stood poised, her hull glis-

tening under a fresh coat of black paint. Above the huge gantry encasing the vessel flew the British Red Ensign, the American Stars and Stripes, and a set of signal flags spelling out "Good Luck."

Just before noon Lord Pirrie, the elderly Chairman of Harland & Wolff, began receiving his Distinguished Guests at the shipyard's main offices on Queen's Road. The owner's party was led, of course, by Joseph Bruce Ismay, Chairman and Managing Director of the White Star Line. His father, Thomas Ismay, had been a towering figure—the man who built White Star from scratch—which might help explain why the son struck some people as autocratic and overly assertive.

Numerically, the Ismay family dominated the owner's party, but only numerically. The truly dominating figure in the group was the great American financier J. Pierpont Morgan, whose fierce, piercing glance could wither any target. In 1902 Morgan had formed the International Mercantile Marine, a huge shipping trust which now controlled the White Star Line. The *Titanic* flew the British flag, but her ownership was about as British as U.S. Steel, another Morgan trust.

Promptly at noon Lord Pirrie led his guests from the offices to the observation stands a few yards away. These had been hastily hammered together and draped with bunting for the occasion. The owner's party filed into a small stand alongside the *Titanic*'s port bow. Other guests joined the press, now 90 strong, in the main stand directly in front of the liner's bow.

His guests seated, Pirrie headed off for a final inspection of the launching gear. He sported a jaunty yachting cap, a fittingly festive touch for the occasion. Today marked not only the launching of the largest ship in the world; it was also his and Lady Pirrie's birthday.

At 12:05 P.M. a red signal flag was hoisted on the *Titanic*'s sternpost, warning the tugs and spectator fleet to stand clear. At 12:10 a rocket was fired, announcing five minutes to go. The pounding of hammers on a dozen last-minute chores ceased. The buzz of conversation in the stands tapered off. The great crowds in the Albert Quay enclosure, at Spencer Basin, in the harbor craft, and on the wharfs and quays all fell silent, as the final minutes ticked away.

At 12:14 another rocket was fired, but for long seconds the *Titanic* still seemed to stand motionless on the stocks. The workers on deck were the first to sense a trace of movement, and they began to cheer. Those on shore took it up, as they too could now see the ship coming to life. A bedlam of whistles added to the din, along with the crack of bracing timbers and the jangle of anchor chains, meant to slow the vessel down once she was afloat. Slowly gathering momentum, she glided smoothly down the ways, lubricated with 3 tons of soft soap, 15 tons of tallow, and 5 tons of tallow mixed with train oil. At 12:15:02—just 62 seconds after she began to move—the *Titanic* was proudly afloat.

While a fleet of tugs nudged her toward the fitting-out berth, Lord Pirrie hosted an intimate luncheon at the shipyard for the Ismay party and Mr. Morgan. Their day was capped by a special treat: at 2:30 they were whisked to the *Titanic*'s sister ship *Olympic*, which had just completed her trials and was lying in Belfast Lough. She would take the Distinguished Guests back to England, giving them a preview of life on the great new vessel they had just seen launched—except that the *Titanic* would be even more magnificent.

Meanwhile most of the dignitaries present at the launching enjoyed a gala luncheon at Belfast's Grand Central Hotel. Besides port officials and visiting firemen, this group included the engineers, naval architects, and technical experts whose expertise enabled the great Edwardian Captains of Industry to put together their grand schemes and designs. These technicians were both underpaid and overworked, and it was a positive bargain if Harland & Wolff could keep them happy with an occasional luncheon of filet de boeuf washed down with Château Larose 1888, as was the case today.

Finally, there was the press. They, too, were given a special luncheon at the Grand Central Hotel, this one hosted by the White Star Line. Speaking for the line, Mr. J. Shelley thanked the journalists for their support, and pointed out that shipbuilding was doing more good for the Anglo-Saxon race than all the chancelleries of Europe combined.

"Hear! Hear!" cried the newsmen, and in a flowery response, the well-known maritime writer Frank T. Bullen praised the modesty of Harland & Wolff in eschewing ceremonial frills like bands and flag-waving. That was "the British way," he noted approvingly.

The proceedings concluded with the entire press corps sending a telegram to Lord Pirrie on the *Olympic,* wishing him and Lady Pirrie a happy birthday, and congratulating them both on the successful trials of the *Olympic* and launch of the *Titanic.*

There was only one sour note. The editor of the *Irish News and Belfast Morning News*—evidently a mythologist—couldn't understand why the ship was named *Ti-tanic.* The Titans, he pointed out in an editorial the following morning, were a mythological race who waged war against Zeus himself to their ultimate ruin. "He smote the strong and daring Titans with thunderbolts; and their final abiding place was in some limbo beneath the lowest depths of the Tartarus." It seemed strange to name this great new ship after a race that "symbolized the vain efforts of mere strength to resist the ordinances of the more 'civilized' order established by Zeus, their triumphant enemy."

The paper finally decided, a little lamely, that the *Titanic* had been apparently named in the spirit of contradiction, that she represented the ultimate triumph of order and modern civilization, and that her builders and owners really stood for a later race of mythological giants who were wiser than their Titanic fathers. In other words, the builders and owners knew best, and they must have had some good reason for this seemingly inappropriate name.

CHAPTER III

Legendary from the Start

The building of the *Titanic*
has created almost as many legends as her sinking. Not
long after *A Night to Remember* was published, several
letters arrived from Ireland explaining the "real" reason
why the ship sank. The trouble could be traced, these
letters said, to the official number—3909 04—given the
Titanic by those Ulstermen who built her. Held up to a
mirror, these figures spell NO POPE. True enough,
provided one fudges the "4" a little.

But a quick check of the records destroys the theory.
The yard number assigned to the *Titanic* by Harland &
Wolff was "401," and her Board of Trade official number was "131,428." Viewed in a mirror, neither of these
numbers says anything at all.

Then there is the legend that the *Titanic* was adver-
tised as "unsinkable." The press, captivated by the iron-
ical implications, has faithfully repeated the story
through the years. Actually, the White Star ads never
made such a claim about either the *Titanic* or her sister

27

ship *Olympic*. All promotion almost invariably used the simple slogan "Largest and finest steamers in the world."

This bit of debunking has now led the inevitable band of *Titanic* revisionists to go much further. "I can find no contemporary evidence that the *Titanic* was regarded as virtually unsinkable until after she had sunk," wrote journalist Philip Howard in the London *Times* in 1981. "With hindsight we have created the myth because it makes a more dramatic metaphor."

He should have looked a little harder. On June 1, 1911, along with its account of the *Titanic*'s launch, the *Irish News and Belfast Morning News* ran a follow-up story headlined TITANIC DESCRIBED. This included a detailed account of the ship's 16 watertight compartments and the electrically controlled doors that connected them. "In the event of an accident, or at any time when it may be considered advisable, the captain can, by simply moving an electric switch, instantly close the doors throughout, practically making the vessel unsinkable."

Later that June the prestigious magazine *Shipbuilder* also described these miracle doors, explaining how they could be closed by merely flicking a switch on the bridge, making the ship "practically unsinkable."

Captain Smith himself believed it. As he explained when he brought over the much smaller *Adriatic* in 1906:

> I cannot imagine any condition which would cause a ship to founder. I cannot conceive of any vital disaster happening to this vessel. Modern shipbuilding has gone beyond that.

So the "unsinkability" of the *Titanic* was not the product of some slick advertising copywriter, nor was it a myth later invented to improve the story. It was the considered opinion of the experts at the time, and it worked its greatest mischief neither before nor after the event, but during the hours of agonizing uncertainty while the tragedy was still unfolding.

"We place absolute confidence in the *Titanic*. We believe that the boat is unsinkable," declared Philip A. S. Franklin, Vice-President of the White Star Line in New York, as the first alarming reports began to drift in around 8 A.M. on April 15.

The *Titanic* could certainly float two or three days, he elaborated around noon. Other experts seemed to agree. Captain Johnson of the American Liner *St. Paul* declared that it was practically impossible for the *Titanic* to sink, because her 15 bulkheads would keep her afloat indefinitely. Actually, the *Titanic* had by now been at the bottom of the sea a good 12 hours.

"I want to say this," Franklin later testified at the U.S. Senate investigation. "During the entire day we considered the ship unsinkable, and it never entered our minds that there had been anything like a serious loss of life."

How close to "unsinkable" really was the *Titanic*? Did she embody the latest engineering techniques? Was she as staunch as man could make her? Did she at least represent what we have now come to call "the state of the art"?

The answer is "No." Far from being a triumph of safe construction, or the best that could be done with the technology available, the *Titanic* was the product of a trend the other way, a trend that for 50 years had seen one safety feature after another sacrificed for competitive reasons.

In 1858 a ship had been built that really did come

close to being unsinkable. This was the *Great Eastern,* a mammoth liner of 19,000 tons and nearly 700 feet in length. She proved a commercial disaster—unwieldy, under-powered, uneconomical, and unlucky—but in one respect she was superb. She brilliantly incorporated every safety feature that could be devised.

The *Great Eastern* was really two ships in one. Two feet, 10 inches, inside her outer hull was a wholly separate inner hull, the two joined together by a network of braces. Like the *Titanic,* she was divided into 16 watertight compartments by 15 transverse bulkheads, but on the *Great Eastern,* the bulkheads ran higher and had no doors. To get from one compartment to another, it was necessary to climb to the bulkhead deck, cross over, and go down the other side. The bulkhead deck was also watertight, with a minimum of hatches and companionways. Finally, the *Great Eastern* had two longitudinal bulkheads extending the whole length of her boiler and engine rooms. This honeycomb of walls and decks gave her a total of some 40–50 separate watertight compartments.

The acid test came on the night of August 27, 1862, two years after she began her trans-Atlantic service. Steaming for New York with 820 passengers, the *Great Eastern* was off Montauk Point, Long Island, when she scraped an uncharted rock, ripping a gash in her outer skin 83 feet long and 9 feet wide. Considering her size, the hole was comparable to the damage that sank the *Titanic.*

But the *Great Eastern* did not go down. She sagged to starboard, but the inner skin held and the engine rooms remained dry. Next morning she limped into New York Harbor under her own steam.

Her survival was a tribute to the engineering genius of her builder, Isambard Kingdom Brunel—and to the mood of the times. The mechanical engineer was the western world's new hero—and no wonder. Twenty years before the building of the *Great Eastern,* the only way to cross the Atlantic was by sailing packet. Slow, cramped, and unpredictable, the trip could take a month. Then, almost overnight it seemed, came these absurd-looking floating "teakettles." Their pistons hissing and clanking, their tall chimneys belching smoke and sparks, their paddle wheels thrashing the waves, they quickly cut the trip to less than ten days. The men who wrought this miracle—the engineers who made steam do their bidding—were deferred to on every question involving the design and construction of these new contraptions. If Brunel wanted his "leviathan" to be the best in every way—size, speed, strength, and safety— that was the way it would be, regardless of cost.

But the engineers did not have the last word for very long. The speed and reliability of the new steamships meant a great surge in trans-Atlantic travel, with profits further fattened by the growing emigrant trade and generous mail contracts. The stakes were high, and by 1873 eleven major lines were fighting for their share. Entrepreneurs and promoters moved in, and the perfect ship was no longer the vessel that best expressed the art of the shipbuilder. It was the ship that made the most money.

Passengers demanded attention; stewards could serve them more easily if doors were cut in the watertight bulkheads. A grand staircase required a spacious opening at every level, making a watertight deck impossible. The sweep of a magnificent dining saloon left no room for bulkheads that might spoil the effect. Stokers could work more efficiently if longitudinal bulkheads were omitted and the bunkers carried clear across the ship. A double hull ate up valuable passenger and cargo space; a double bottom would be enough.

One by one the safety precautions that marked the *Great Eastern* were chipped away in the interests of a more competitive ship. There were exceptions of course—the *Mauretania* and *Lusitania* had to meet Admiralty specifications—but the *Olympic* and *Titanic* were more typical. When the "unsinkable" *Titanic* was completed in 1912, she matched the *Great Eastern* in only one respect: she, too, had 15 transverse watertight bulkheads.

But even this was misleading. The *Great Eastern's* bulkheads were carried 30 feet above the waterline; the *Titanic's* bulkheads, only 10 feet. Even her vaunted system of watertight doors that could be closed from the bridge "by simply moving a switch" fell short of its promise. Only 12 doors at the very bottom of the ship could be closed this way. The rest (some 20 or 30) had to be closed by hand. On the night of the collision some were; some weren't. Some were even closed, then opened again to make it easier to rig the pumps.

Why, then, was such a vulnerable ship considered by the owners themselves to be virtually unsinkable? Partly, it was because the *Titanic* would indeed float with any two compartments flooded, and the White Star Line couldn't imagine anything worse than a collision at the juncture of two compartments. But there was another reason, too, why the owners were lulled into complacency. This was because the ship *looked* so safe. Her huge bulk, her tiers of decks rising one atop the other, her 29 boilers, her luxurious fittings—all seemed to spell "permanence." The appearance of safety was mistaken for safety itself.

The *Titanic* was indeed a magnificent sight as she left Belfast on April 2, 1912, and headed for Southampton, where she would begin her service on the North Atlantic run. At 46,328 tons, she was the largest ship in the world—only a trifle bigger than her sister ship *Olympic,* but 50% larger than any other liner afloat. With ships increasing in size so dramatically, her vast bulk inevitably led to still more legends: that she had a golf course . . . that she carried a small herd of dairy cows to supply fresh milk . . . that she was a half-mile long. The *Titanic* boasted none of these features; in fact, she was quite similar to the *Olympic,* which had already been in service for a year. White Star's problem was how to give the new ship a little extra glamour when both vessels had basically the same structure.

The company solved this problem brilliantly with two new amenities that required a minimum of structural change. First, a set of 28 splendid staterooms were installed on B Deck, more lavish than any on the *Olympic* and complete with large windows (not portholes) that looked out directly on the sea. Most of these rooms were interconnecting and could be turned into suites of any size. Each was painstakingly decorated in a different period style—Louis XVI, Early Dutch, Regency, and so on. Two suites even had private promenade decks done in half-timbered Tudor.

The second innovation was even more arresting. A section of the Second Class Promenade Deck was appro-

priated for a dazzling new First Class attraction: a genuine French "sidewalk" café, complete with genuine
French waiters. By now the veteran Atlantic traveler was
bored by mere paneled magnificence—one more ornate
lounge would have made no impression—but the addition of this bright, airy café with its Continental chic
(especially on a staid British ship) was sensational.

As a final touch, the forward half of the Promenade
Deck was glassed in, giving the First Class passengers
extra shelter in bad weather and, incidentally, marking
the *Titanic* as a step ahead of her sister ship *Olympic*.

Both the Café Parisien and the new "special staterooms" stirred great attention as the *Titanic* prepared to
sail on her maiden voyage, April 10. They stamped her
as the most luxurious ship on the Atlantic—at least until
next year, when an immense new German liner, already
taking shape at Hamburg, would enter the unending
struggle for maritime supremacy.

CHAPTER IV

Had Ships Gotten Too Big for Captain Smith?

As I recall, on the day it sailed, all England was merry in the celebration of a holiday for the occasion. Flags flying in the breeze in every city and hamlet. There was the inevitable speech-making. That gloriously martial air, "Britannia Rules the Waves," was the mighty theme-song of the day. . . .

So the Reverend Wilfred G. Hurley described the *Titanic*'s maiden sailing, April 10, 1912, in a little pamphlet published 37 years later by the Missionary Society of St. Paul the Apostle. It is a familiar picture, handed down by countless writers through the years.

Actually, the White Star Line made very little of the *Titanic*'s departure. There were no bands, no speeches, no flag-waving. The only touch out of the ordinary was an immense crowd. Southampton was a seafaring town, and it seemed that the whole city wanted to watch the greatest ship in the world start off on her maiden voyage. But it was a knowledgeable crowd, almost professionally observant, and not at all given to singing or cheering.

Yet, the departure did have its excitement. While the *Titanic* was casting off, promptly at 12 noon, seven members of the "black gang," as the stokers and firemen were called, came racing down the dock hoping to scramble aboard. They had gone ashore for a last pint and somehow lingered too long. Now they stood by an open ship's gangway, arguing with the officer on duty there. He clearly wanted no part of them—they were too late, and that was that. Frustrated, the little group melted into the crowd, cursing this rotten turn in their luck.

Imperceptibly, the gulf widened between the *Titanic* and the dock; she was under weigh at last. Assisted by six tugs, she slowly crept out of the slip and into the channel of the River Test. Here her enormous bulk was maneuvered to the left, toward open water and ultimately the sea.

As she moved down the channel, now under her own power, the *Titanic* came abreast of two smaller liners moored to the quay on the left. These were the White Star's *Oceanic* and the American Line's *New York,* idled by a coal strike that had paralyzed most of British shipping for weeks. Warped side by side, with the *New York* on the outside, they made the narrow channel even more narrow.

The *Titanic* glided on, steaming at about six knots. As she drew opposite the *New York,* there was a sudden series of sharp cracks, like pistol shots. One after another, all six of the lines tying the *New York* to the *Oceanic* snapped. Drawn by some inexorable force, the American Liner began drifting toward the huge *Titanic*. For a moment a collision seemed certain, as the stern of the *New York* swung to within three or four feet of the port quarter of the *Titanic*.

Quick thinking saved the day. The tug *Vulcan,* one of the small fleet escorting the *Titanic,* darted to the danger spot. Her skipper, Captain Gale, passed a line to the *New York*'s stern, and with much puffing and straining, the *Vulcan* managed to slow the vessel's drift. At the same time Captain Smith on the *Titanic*'s bridge nudged his port engine forward, creating a wash that helped push the *New York* clear. There was still plenty of danger, for the American Liner was completely adrift without any steam up, and she slid at an angle down the narrow corridor of water between the *Titanic* and the *Oceanic* with only inches to spare. Miraculously there was no contact, and finally the errant *New York* was corralled and towed to another berth, safely out of the way. The channel was clear at last, and the *Titanic* headed for open water.

Covering the incident, the *Southampton Times and Hampshire Gazette* didn't know why it had happened. The paper merely explained that the passing of the *Titanic* had caused the *New York* to break away "by some means or other." But of one thing the editors were sure: the near-collision was not a case of bad shiphandling by Captain Smith of the *Titanic:* "From the moment she began to move from her berth she was under absolute control, and she passed out of the dock not only majestically, but also smoothly and calmly. If anything, she was proceeding more slowly than the *Olympic* usually does, and she turned her nose toward the sea with the greatest ease."

It was only natural to rush to Captain Smith's support. He was at the pinnacle of a brilliant career. Going to sea as an apprentice on a clipper ship in 1869, he gradually worked his way up the ladder, joining White Star in 1880 as fourth officer on the old *Celtic.* By 1887 he was captain of the *Republic,* and since then he had commanded no fewer than 17 White Star vessels.

All the time he honed the qualities that made the trans-Atlantic captain such a unique breed. He was a superb seaman. He was a firm disciplinarian, but fair and popular with his crews. He was a splendid inn-keeper, gradually building up a loyal clientele of devoted passengers. Here a personal note is perhaps revealing. Around the turn of the century my mother, torn by affairs of the heart, was urged by her father to take a trip abroad to "sort things out." He didn't care where she went, how long she stayed, or what ship she took—as long as she sailed with Captain Smith. On occasional business trips he himself had sailed with Smith and swore by the man.

Mother accordingly set off on the *Baltic,* which was Captain Smith's ship at the time. She solved her problems before they were out of sight of Ambrose Lightship; so it was simply a trip across the ocean and back—still on the *Baltic;* still sailing with Captain Smith.

He was a big man, gray-bearded, barrel-chested, and with the autocratic look of an officer who might thunder orders from the bridge. Actually, he was extremely soft-spoken, rarely raised his voice, and smiled easily. His whole appeal was low-key. Bringing the *Adriatic* over on her maiden voyage in 1907, he told the New York press:

> When anyone asks me how I can best describe my experiences of nearly 40 years at sea, I merely say "uneventful." I have never been in an accident of any sort worth speaking about. I never saw a wreck and have never been wrecked, nor was I ever in any predicament that threatened to end in disaster of any sort.

"Uneventful" paid off. Captain Smith was the obvious choice to command the great new *Olympic* when she entered service in 1911. She was nearly twice as big as any ship he had handled before, but it seemed only coincidence when an odd mishap occurred almost right away.

Arriving in New York, June 21, on her maiden voyage, the *Olympic* received the traditional welcome of whistle blasts and flag-dips as she moved up the North River to Pier 59, especially lengthened to receive her. Here 12 tugs took over, nursing her into her slip, with an occasional assist from the *Olympic*'s engines. The tug *O. L. Hallenbeck* was standing by near the liner's stern, when a sudden reverse burst of the *Olympic*'s starboard propeller sucked it against the ship, cutting off the *Hallenbeck*'s stern frame, rudder, and wheel shaft.

Who gave the order to reverse the starboard engine? The *Olympic* was under the pilot's control, but the captain is always responsible for his ship, and Captain Smith was no exception. Information is scanty. The press tended to treat the affair as good clean fun—the *Times* called the crash a "playful touch"—and only the tug's owner seemed really annoyed. He sued White Star for $10,000, a significant sum in those days. White Star responded with a countersuit, and ultimately both cases were dismissed for lack of evidence. Nobody saw the incident for what it really was: a disturbing lesson in the difficulty of managing a steamer of the *Olympic*'s unprecedented size. It turned even the most experienced seaman into an inexperienced novice.

Another incident drove home the point three months later. Shortly after noon, September 20, as the *Olympic* began her fifth voyage to New York, she fell in with the Royal Navy cruiser *Hawke* in the narrow channel of a tricky body of water called Spithead, off the Isle of Wight. The *Olympic* had seven times the tonnage of the *Hawke*, and was nearly three times as long.

The two vessels were going in roughly the same direction on courses that were at first converging, then parallel, with the *Hawke* off the *Olympic*'s starboard side. They were soon only 200 yards apart. Both were going at about 15 knots, with the *Hawke* at first overhauling the *Olympic*, then beginning to drop behind as the liner opened up her speed.

Suddenly, without warning, the *Hawke* veered hard to port and headed straight for the *Olympic*'s starboard quarter. It took only a few seconds. At 12:46 P.M. there was a crash like a thunderclap as the cruiser rammed the liner's hull. Luckily no one was killed, but the *Hawke*'s bow was badly crumpled, and the *Olympic* received a double gash toward the stern, flooding two compartments and damaging her starboard propeller. Her passengers were taken off by tender, and the liner limped back to Southampton and then to Belfast for six weeks of repairs.

The obvious villain was the *Hawke*. The *Olympic*'s passengers, interviewed by the press, were almost unanimous in declaring that the cruiser suddenly and for no apparent reason turned and rammed their ship. The *Hawke*'s captain, some said, must have been "crazy." As for Captain Smith, all agreed that he was "the best on the Atlantic."

The case eventually went to court, where the Admiralty came up with a startling defense that went beyond such standard questions as who had the right of way, and whether the ships were on "parallel" or "converging" courses. Bolstered by experts who had experimented with small models in tanks, the Admiralty argued that far from being the transgressor, the *Hawke* was the innocent victim. She had been helplessly drawn into the side of the *Olympic* by hydrodynamic forces over which she had no control. When a ship's hull is moving forward, the experts explained, it pushes out on either side a large amount of water. This displaced water then surges back toward the stern and into the vessel's wake. In doing so, it draws or sucks in any smaller object that happens to be afloat nearby. The pull increases with the size, speed, and proximity of the larger moving hull. Here, the pull was irresistible. The 45,000-ton *Olympic* was much too close, considering the speed she was making as she began drawing ahead of the 7,500-ton *Hawke*.

The Court listened and was convinced. The *Hawke* was cleared, and the *Olympic* held to blame for the collision.

"Thoroughly unsatisfactory" was the reaction of *Nautical Magazine,* the accepted spokesman for officers of the British merchant service. The editors were especially indignant about the experts' use of models to prove the hydrodynamic forces at work. How could the movement of "light toys" floating in a tank prove anything about two vessels "weighing thousands of tons" in the actual sea? "When all is said, the *practical* seaman will dismiss these model experiments as useless and only fit for the consideration of the Admiralty lawyers."

The White Star Line evidently agreed. Arguably Captain Smith was off the hook anyhow, since the *Olympic* was under pilot at the time, but a captain is always responsible for his ship, and there were plenty of ways that the owners could have shown their displeasure, if they were unhappy about his performance.

Instead, they promoted him. Early in 1912, Captain Smith was named to command the new and even bigger *Titanic,* flagship of the fleet. He would take her over and back on her maiden voyage, and then retire. He was now 59, and this would be a way of thanking him for his years of loyal service.

Sailing day, and the *Titanic*'s near-collision with the *New York* showed that Captain Smith, too, had rejected the Court's reasoning in the *Olympic-Hawke* case. After all, the two incidents were almost identical: the same captain, the same pilot, the same interaction of hulls, the same result. If Captain Smith had believed there was anything to the suction theory, he would hardly have let it happen twice.

This second episode convinced the whole shipping world that the suction theory was valid after all. Clearly those scientists experimenting with models weren't just playing with bathtub toys "in pleasant remembrance of younger days," as *Nautical Magazine* unkindly put it. Presumably Captain Smith got the message, too, but a nagging question remains: how much else was there to learn about these huge new liners that were so different from the ships he was used to?

Until 1911, Captain Smith's largest ship had only half the tonnage of the *Olympic* and *Titanic*. For most of his career, his ships had been less than 500 feet long; the *Olympic* and *Titanic* were nearly 900 feet. Did he fully appreciate the difference? Did he realize how much longer it would take to stop a 46,000-ton ship going 22 knots? Or how many more seconds it would take one of these new giants to answer the helm? Or how much wider her turning circle would be?

Certainly the *Titanic*'s trials could not have been very helpful. They took up only half a day in Belfast Lough. According to most accounts, the *Titanic* simply steamed a few miles, made some twists and turns (Fifth Officer Lowe said only one big U-turn), then back to Belfast again to put the Harland & Wolff technicians ashore. This done, she headed for Southampton to begin her regular service. The trials seem amazingly perfunctory when compared, for instance, to the trials of the liner *United States,* which lasted six weeks.

Captain Smith, too, seems to have felt that something more was needed. He did a surprising thing as the *Titanic,* after a brief stop at Cherbourg, steamed toward Queenstown early on the morning of April 11. In a little while there would be the hurly-burly of taking on hundreds of Irish emigrants, then the pressures of keeping schedule across the Atlantic. Now, he had a quiet moment to tie up a few loose ends. The *Titanic* began practicing turns, leaving a wake of lazy S's, as Captain Smith continued to educate himself on the ways of his immense new command.

CHAPTER V

"Our Coterie"

As the *Titanic* headed out to sea, and the green hills of Ireland faded into the dusk astern, her First Class passengers busied themselves with the ritual that invariably opened every Atlantic voyage; they studied the Passenger List, looking for old friends or familiar names that might be worth cultivating. The list was neatly printed in booklet form and slipped under the stateroom door by the steward or "Buttons," as the bellboys were called.

It makes as fascinating reading today as it did the first night out. Like stars in a Broadway production, the big names are all there: the Astors, of course, along with the Wideners, Thayers, and others prominent in Society. They would be enough to adorn any important occasion in 1912, but what made the *Titanic* special was the presence of leaders in so many different fields: the artist Frank Millet; the editor W. T. Stead; the writer Jacques Futrelle; the theatrical producer Henry B. Harris; President Taft's military aide Archie Butt; the elderly phi-

lanthropist Isidor Straus and his wife, Ida. Also noted
(but not named) were 31 personal maids and valets, just
in case the ship's army of stewards and stewardesses
weren't enough to satisfy every need.

What makes the list even more intriguing today are
certain inaccuracies and omissions. It included, for instance, the name of at least one man who wasn't on
board at all. Frank Carlson was an American visiting
France who hoped to catch the *Titanic* home. Driving to
Cherbourg in his own car, he had the misfortune to
break down, and by the time repairs were made, he had
missed the boat. But his name remained on the Passenger List, and later on the casualty list, when he failed to
answer the roll call of survivors. Sixty years afterward
his family were still trying to correct the error.

Others were not on the Passenger List, but definitely
on the *Titanic*. Mrs. Henry B. Cassebeer boarded the
liner as a Second Class passenger. She was an impecu-
nious young widow, but a very experienced traveler.
Knowing that expensive cabins often went begging in
the off-season, she visited the Purser's Office. At the cost
of a few pounds under the counter, she upgraded herself from Second Class to one of the best First Class
staterooms on the ship.

Flushed with success, she ran into Chief Purser
McElroy a little later and playfully suggested that she be
seated at the Captain's table. "I'll do better than that,"
McElroy gallantly replied. "I'll have you seated at *my*
table!"

Sir Cosmo and Lady Duff Gordon were two other
names missing from the Passenger List but definitely on
the *Titanic*. For some reason they were traveling as "Mr.

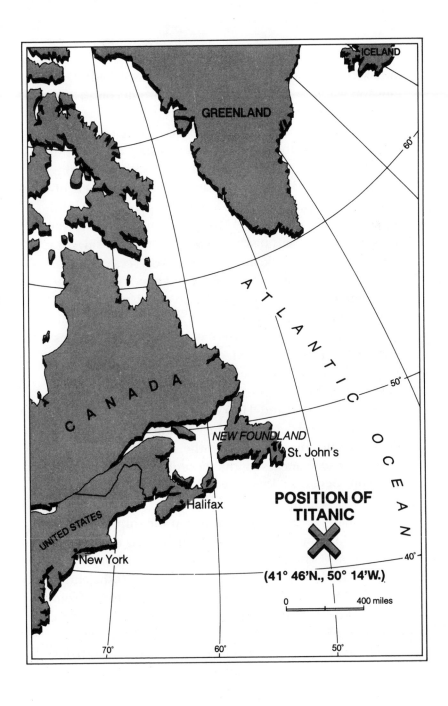

ICELAND

GREENLAND

60°

ATLANTIC

50°

CANADA

NEW FOUNDLAND

St. John's

OCEAN

POSITION OF
TITANIC

Halifax

✖

40°

UNITED STATES

New York

(41° 46'N., 50° 14'W.)

0   400 miles

70°   60°   50°

and Mrs. Morgan"—an odd decision, since Lady Duff Gordon was one of Society's most important couturières and lived by publicity.

More understandable was the decision of George Rosenshine and Maybelle Thorne to be listed as "Mr. and Mrs. G. Thorne." They were not married but traveling together, and in the Edwardian era, appearances were often more important than reality. Appearances also played a part in the case of "Miss E. Rosenbaum." She was a fashion stylist, and it simply seemed better business to anglicize her name. So although listed correctly, she was generally known as Edith Russell, and that is the way she has come down to us in most survivor accounts.

Three other passengers found it absolutely essential to travel incognito. They were professional cardsharps, hoping to make a maiden voyage killing. Obviously it was safer to use an assumed name; so George (Boy) Bradley was listed as "George Brayton"; C. H. Romaine as "C. Rolmane"; and Harry (Kid) Homer as "E. Haven." There's evidence that the well-known gambler Jay Yates was also on board, using the alias "J. H. Rogers." Neither name appears on the Passenger List, but a farewell note signed by Rogers was later handed to a survivor on the sloping Boat Deck.

One shady figure definitely not on the ship was Alvin Clarence Thomas, a con man later known as "Titanic Thompson," who achieved a certain notoriety as a witness to the slaying of the gambler Arnold Rothstein in 1929. It was generally assumed that the alias came from Thompson's having plied his trade on the *Titanic,* but this is not so—he was only nine at the time. Actually, the name was an appropriate reference to several disastrous plunges taken when the stakes were high.

While the presence of this or that particular individual could be argued, there's no doubt that a number of cardsharps were indeed on the *Titanic,* and in fact on almost every express liner plying the Atlantic at the time. The combination of rich, bored passengers, easily made shipboard friendships, and the ambience of the smoking room provided the perfect climate for "sportsmen," as the gamblers were politely called.

The wonder is that the lines didn't do more to protect their ordinary passengers. The veteran gamblers were familiar figures to most of the pursers and smoking room stewards: were they being bribed to keep quiet? Undoubtedly there were occasional payoffs, but the real source of trouble seems to have been the steamship companies themselves. They didn't want to take any step that implied they might be responsible for their patrons' losses. Nor were all high-stake games dishonest; there was always the legal danger of a false charge. It was safer not to get involved.

On the *Titanic* there was only one low-keyed warning. This was a mild little insert, planted opposite the first page of the Passenger List:

SPECIAL NOTICE

The attention of the Managers has been called to the fact that certain persons, believed to be Professional Gamblers, are in the habit of traveling to and fro in Atlantic Steamships.

In bringing this to the knowledge of Travelers the Managers, while not wishing in the slightest degree to interfere with the freedom of action of Patrons of the White Star Line, desire to invite their assistance in discouraging Games of Chance, as being

likely to afford these individuals special opportunities for taking unfair advantage of others.

Along with the deceptions, the *Titanic*'s Passenger List
had its share of printer's errors—unintended, but no
less misleading to browsers then and now. "H. Bjornstrom," for instance, was really H. Bjornstrom Steffanson, a wealthy young Swedish businessman, whose
father seemed to own all the wood pulp in Sweden.
Steffanson was a lieutenant in the Swedish Army Reserve, but his eyes were set on Wall Street. This was his
third trip to New York in two years, and already he was
well on his way to making a small fortune of his own.
    Also on the list was Mrs. Churchill "Cardell"—whose
last name should have been spelled "Candee." In an era
when genteel ladies were regarded as helpless creatures
to be protected by solicitous males, Helen Churchill
Candee had already jumped the traces with a book called
How Women May Earn a Living. Published in 1900, it was
full of crisp, breezy advice. Mrs. Candee had something
to say about almost any subject, and other books soon
followed: a western called *An Oklahoma Romance;* a cul-
tural guide called *Decorative Styles and Periods;* and a history of tapestry, just finished and due to be published in
the fall.
    But it was not her literary career that put Helen
Candee on the *Titanic;* it was a personal emergency. Her
son had been hurt in an aeroplane accident—a novelty
in 1912 that vicariously added to her own glamour—
and she was hurrying to his bedside.
    Meanwhile she must make the best of things. It was
the off-season, and some 87 unattached men were in
First Class. It did not take long for several of them to

notice the handsome woman traveling alone, who could usually be found reading in her deck chair on the Promenade Deck, forward. For her part, Mrs. Candee always took two chairs—"one for myself and the other for callers, or for self-protection." No less than six shipboard swains were soon vying for that extra chair.

Of them all, she knew only Colonel Gracie, slightly. An amateur military historian, he had just finished a detailed Civil War battle history, *The Truth about Chickamauga.* Now he was crossing the ocean and back, to get it out of his system. Two others of the group had been recommended to her by mutual friends: Hugh Woolner, son of a noted English sculptor; and Edward A. Kent, a well-connected Buffalo architect. The rest were complete strangers, to be fixed in her mind the way one does with shipboard acquaintances. Clinch Smith was the Long Island socialite who kept polo ponies and lived mostly in Paris; Bjornstrom Steffanson was the dashing Swedish reserve officer; E. P. Colley was the roly-poly Irishman who laughed a lot but said little.

They were all dazzled by Mrs. Candee, and she in turn "felt divinely flattered to be in such company." Coming on deck one day after lunch, she found them already waiting by her chairs. "We are here to amuse you," one of them gushed. "All of us have the same thought, which is that you must never be alone." Together, they formed one of those groups that sometimes happen on an Atlantic crossing, where the chemistry is just right and the members are inseparable . . . at least until last night out. To Colonel Gracie, they were "our coterie."

The days glided by, one blending into another to form a seamless whole. The weather was always sunny, the ocean calm. In past crossings Colonel Gracie had made a point of keeping in shape, but this time he found "our coterie" so enjoyable that he forgot about exercise.

Sunday, April 14, Gracie decided that he must get back on some sort of regimen. He bounced out of bed for a pre-breakfast warm-up with Fred Wright, the ship's squash pro. Then a plunge in the swimming pool, and up for a big breakfast. Later he attended divine service, conducted by Captain Smith, and joined the rest of those present in the "Prayer for Those at Sea."

Early afternoon, the weather suddenly turned cold. Most of the passengers stayed inside, writing letters and catching up on their reading. Gracie finished Mary Johnson's *Old Dominion* and returned it to the ship's library. Later he cornered Isidor Straus, on whom he had foisted a copy of *The Truth about Chickamauga*. The book strikes one reader as 462 pages of labored minutiae, but Mr. Straus was famous for his tact; he assured the Colonel that he had read it with "intense interest."

Despite the cold, Mrs. Candee and Hugh Woolner decided to explore the ship. A door on the starboard side of the Boat Deck was open, and hearing some clicking sounds, they looked in. "Come in, come right in and try your strength," called a cheery English voice. It was T. W. McCawley, the gym instructor, a bouncy little man in white flannels, eager to show off his domain. For the next hour they raced the stationary bicycles, rode the mechanical horses, and even took a turn on the "camel," which McCawley said was good for the liver.

But it was getting colder all the time, and they decided to go down to the lounge for tea. They settled into a green velvet settee before a glowing grate, and it reminded Helen Candee of coming back home to a fireplace after a frosty afternoon ride over the fields. Stewards arrived with steaming pots of tea and plates piled high with buttered toast, and she sensed a general feeling of total well-being and contentment—rare indeed since her son's accident.

The spell was broken by the bugle to dress for dinner. For the next hour, First Class seemed almost empty, as "our coterie" and the others struggled behind closed stateroom doors with hundreds of shirt studs and thousands of hairpins. Every steward and stewardess—every personal maid and valet—was mobilized to help.

Dinner was the social high point of the day. The elite dined in the À la Carte Restaurant, but the main dining saloon on D Deck had glitter enough. The scene might have been the Ritz in London or Sherry's in New York, with the men in white tie (except for a few daring souls in tuxedo), and the ladies shining in pale satin and clinging gauze. Tonight even the impoverished Mrs. Cassebeer looked superb, resplendent in the only snappy evening gown she had.

There's no record of what Mrs. Candee was wearing, but it's a safe guess that she looked irresistible to her six devoted swains. After a dinner of filet mignon Lili, they took a table together in the adjoining Reception Room for coffee and the nightly concert by the *Titanic*'s band.

The band has become so hallowed in memory that it seems almost blasphemous to say anything critical about its music. Nevertheless, there were those in "our coterie" who did feel that it was poor on its Wagner, while others said that the violin was weak. True or not, Wallace

Hartley and his men were immensely popular with the passengers, and always willing to play any request. Tonight they played some Puccini for Mrs. Candee and a little Dvorak for Hugh Woolner.

Colonel Gracie, who never recognized any number the band played now or later, used the concert as an opportunity to circulate among the crowded little tables that filled the room. He was an indefatigable celebrity collector, and liked to mention his Union Club membership and St. Paul's School background. One can imagine people wincing at his approach but putting up with him anyhow, for he was kind, courtly, and certainly meant well.

Tonight the Colonel had fewer targets than usual, for the truly big names were dining in the À la Carte Restaurant up on B Deck, where the Wideners were giving a small dinner for Captain Smith. Yet there were still plenty of attractive tables, and Gracie felt that the ladies never looked lovelier. Around 9:30 he decided to break off the evening and retire. It was still early, but it had been a long day—all that squash, swimming, and exercises in the gym—and he had reserved the squash court for another session early the following morning.

By 11:00 the rest of the crowd in the Reception Room was breaking up too, and the band finished the evening with the "Tales of Hoffmann." Soon the big Jacobean room was completely empty, except for one remaining table. Mrs. Candee and "our coterie" were going as strong as ever. But even they felt the emptiness of the room and decided to look for some place cozier.

Somebody suggested the Café Parisien, all the way aft on B Deck. It was the showpiece of the ship, stylish but intimate. Certainly there ought to be some life there. But all they found was one other party, presided over by Archie Butt, President Taft's military aide.

And it was so cold. Mrs. Candee drew her scarf close, but it made little difference. They ordered hot drinks, and a waiter appeared with a tray of grog, steaming Scotch and lemon, and (for Bjornstrom Steffanson) a hot lemonade. Even these emergency measures didn't help, and around 11:20 Mrs. Candee reluctantly went below, where there was at least an electric heater in her stateroom.

Colley also drifted off and the four remaining members of "our coterie" now went up to the smoking room, just above on A Deck. This was a male sanctuary where the ship's night owls customarily gathered and which was bound to be warm. Someone produced a pack of cards, and the foursome began to play a rather light-hearted game of bridge. There were other tables of bridge nearby, including one carefully organized by George Brayton and two of his sporting cronies. The fourth at this table was Howard Case, London Manager of the Vacuum Oil Company. Case had been selected as the sharps' next pigeon.

Several other groups sat around simply talking, and one lone traveler—Spencer Silverthorne of St. Louis—buried himself in a big leather chair, idly reading Owen Wister's *The Virginian*. It was now nearly 11:40 P.M., and the hum of conversation blended with the steady throb of the engines far below.

Suddenly an interruption. As Hugh Woolner recalled it a few days later in a letter to a friend, "There came a heavy grinding sort of a shock, beginning far ahead of us in the bows and rapidly passing along the ship and away under our feet."

It was not severe, but enough to spill gambler Harry Romaine's drink. Everyone sprang up, and several of the more curious—including Woolner and Steffanson—darted through the swinging doors aft and onto the open Promenade Deck. Steffanson's eyes couldn't adjust to the sudden darkness fast enough, but he heard one of the others call out, "We hit an iceberg—there it is!"

CHAPTER VI

"Everything Was Against Us"

The bridge was as surprised as the gentlemen in the smoking room. How could the *Titanic* have collided with an iceberg so suddenly, so unexpectedly? Second Officer Lightoller wasn't on the bridge at the time, but he was senior surviving officer, and at the British Inquiry (technically the Wreck Commissioner's Court) he had an almost mystical explanation:

> Of course, we know now the extraordinary combination of circumstances that existed at that time which you would not meet again in 100 years; that they should all have existed just on that particular night shows, of course, that everything was against us.

Pressed to particularize, Lightoller pointed out that there was no moon, no wind, no swell. The Court did not seem overly impressed, but the notion has persisted that the accident was of the one-in-a-million variety, that it couldn't have been foreseen, and that the lost liner was, in fact, a helpless victim of fate.

Was she really? To find the answer, we must start back on the afternoon of April 12 as the *Titanic*—one day out of Queenstown—steamed westward across a calm, sunny sea. Around sunset a wireless message arrived from the French Liner *La Touraine* warning of ice ahead. Captain Smith gave the position to Fourth Officer Boxhall, and Boxhall noted it on the map in the chart room, but it was over a thousand miles away and far to the north of the *Titanic*'s track—no need to worry.

The wireless was quiet on the 13th, but late that night the *Titanic* met the Furness Withy Liner *Rappahannock*, eastbound from Halifax to London. She had recently encountered heavy pack ice, twisting her rudder and denting her bow. Now, as the two ships passed within signaling distance, the *Rappahannock* warned the *Titanic* by blinker of the danger ahead. The great White Star Liner, decks blazing with light, flashed back a brief acknowledgment and hurried on into the night.

Sunday, April 14, and the wireless brought a spate of fresh warnings. At 9 A.M. (*Titanic* time) the Cunard Liner *Caronia* reported "bergs, growlers, and field ice in 42°N, from 49° to 51°W." At 11:40 the Dutch liner *Noordam* also reported "much ice" in roughly the same position, and at 1:42 P.M. the White Star Liner *Baltic* reported "icebergs and large quantity of field ice in 41°51′N, 49°9′W"—about 250 miles ahead.

At 1:45 P.M. still another ice message arrived—the fourth of the day. The German liner *Amerika* reported passing two large icebergs at 41°27′N, 50°8′W. The *Amer-*

ika's message was addressed to the U.S. Hydrographic Office in Washington, but this was beyond her own range; so, in the custom of the times, she asked the *Titanic* to relay it. This the *Titanic* did, thus adding her own voice to the chorus of warnings.

Nothing more till 7:30 P.M.; then a fifth message, this one from the Leyland Liner *California,* position 42°3′N, 49°9′W: "Three large bergs five miles to southward of us." The ice was now only 50 miles ahead.

Finally, at 9:40 P.M., the Atlantic Transport Liner *Mesaba:* "Lat. 42°N to 41°25′N, Longitude 40°W to 50°30′W, saw much heavy pack ice and great number large icebergs, also field ice." The *Titanic* was already in the rectangle blocked out by this warning.

Put together, the six messages indicated an enormous belt of ice stretching some 78 miles directly across the big ship's path.

But the messages were not "put together." If the recollections of the four surviving officers are any guide, most of the warnings went unnoticed on the bridge. Fourth Officer Boxhall, who was always Captain Smith's choice for marking the ship's chart, could only remember pricking off the *La Touraine*'s sighting on April 12.

Of the six ice messages received on the 14th, the day of the collision, there is firm information about only the first two. The *Caronia*'s sighting, received at 9 A.M., appears to have been noted by Boxhall. Third Officer Pitman distinctly remembered seeing him jot the single word "ice" on a slip of paper, with the *Caronia*'s sighting underneath, and then tuck the slip into a frame above the chart room table. Other officers recalled seeing the same sighting pricked off on the chart—also Boxhall's work. And around 12:45 Captain Smith showed the complete *Caronia* message to Second Officer Lightoller, senior officer on the bridge at the time.

About an hour later Captain Smith had the *Baltic*'s warning, too, but there's no evidence that he showed it to anybody on the bridge. Instead, he took it with him as he started down for lunch about 1:30. On the Promenade Deck he ran into Bruce Ismay, who was taking a pre-lunch constitutional. They exchanged greetings, and the Captain handed the Managing Director the *Baltic*'s message as a matter of interest. Ismay glanced at it, stuffed it in his pocket, and went on down to lunch.

He still had it late in the afternoon when he ran into Mrs. Thayer and Mrs. Ryerson, two of the most socially prominent ladies aboard. Ismay, who liked to remind people who he was, lost no time producing the *Baltic* message and reading them the titillating news about icebergs ahead.

Coming out of the smoking room that evening just before dinner, he again met Captain Smith. The Captain asked if Ismay still had the message, explaining that he wanted to post it for his officers to read. Ismay fished it out of his pocket and returned it without any further conversation. Then the two men continued down to the À la Carte Restaurant—Ismay to dine alone with the ship's surgeon, old Dr. O'Laughlin; Smith to join the small party the Wideners were giving in his honor. There's no evidence that the *Baltic*'s information was ever noted on the bridge before the whole affair became academic.

As for the four other ice messages received on the

14th—those from the *Noordam*, *Amerika*, *Californian*, and *Mesaba*—none of them were remembered by any of the surviving officers. The *Noordam*'s warning was acknowledged by Captain Smith, but what he did with it nobody knows. The *Californian*'s message was received by Second Wireless Operator Harold Bride, who testified that he took it to the bridge but didn't know whom he gave it to. The *Amerika* and *Mesaba* warnings were received by First Wireless Operator John Phillips, but what happened to them remains a mystery.

Almost any student of the *Titanic* knows by heart the famous scene where a weary Jack Phillips tucks the *Mesaba*'s warning under a paperweight and goes on working off his backlog of commercial traffic. Yet there's very little evidence to support the story. Lightoller said Phillips told him so while they were clinging to an upturned collapsible boat after the sinking, but nobody else on the collapsible remembered such a conversation. Even Lightoller never mentioned it at the hearings, although it was vitally important and would have helped White Star, which he was trying to do. Nor did Lightoller mention the incident to Fourth Officer Boxhall, while they were on the *Carpathia* going over together every detail of the disaster. Boxhall never heard of the *Mesaba* until he reached New York. The story first emerged in Lightoller's memoirs, 25 years later, where it should be accorded the latitude normally granted an old sea dog reminiscing.

The *Mesaba* message remains a mystery. Perhaps it did end up under the paperweight, but it seems equally possible that sometime after Lightoller went off duty Phillips passed it on to the bridge, where it received the

same attention given the warnings from the *Noordam,*
Amerika, and *Californian*—which was none at all.

What went wrong? To begin with, there seems to have
been little coordination between the radio room and the
bridge. The procedure for handling incoming messages
was fuzzy at best. Any message affecting the navigation
of the ship was meant to go straight to the bridge, but
Phillips and Bride were no navigators; the jumble of
longitudes and latitudes meant nothing to them. Their
method of handling a message really depended on how
it was addressed, rather than what it was about.

If the message was addressed to Captain Smith, one
of the operators would take it directly to the Captain
and hand it to him personally. If addressed simply to
the ship, it might be delivered by a messenger, and to
anyone on duty on the bridge. If sent just to be relayed
on, like the *Amerika*'s alert to the Hydrographic Office in
Washington, there seems to have been no standard
practice at all.

Some messages were even picked up by eavesdrop-
ping, and their handling was left to the operator's dis-
cretion. The *Californian*'s warning, for instance, was
addressed to the liner *Antillian.* Bride just happened to
catch it, jotted it down, and took it to the bridge himself—but never knew whom he gave it to.

Nor does there seem to have been any clear-cut procedure for handling the messages once they reached the
bridge. According to Third Officer Pitman, every captain had his own system, but it's hard to explain the
system on the *Titanic.* Of the three messages addressed
to Captain Smith personally, the *Caronia*'s was posted,
the *Noordam*'s can't be traced, and the *Baltic*'s ended up

in Bruce Ismay's pocket. Of the rest, there's no record
that they were ever seen by any officer on the bridge.
As a result, some important information was missed
altogether. The *Titanic's* surviving officers all thought
the ice lay to the north of the track, but the *Amerika* and
Mesaba warnings clearly placed it to the south as well.
Nor did the officers appear to understand the nature of
the danger. Third Officer Pitman thought there was
only a berg or two; Lightoller also worried about "small
ice and growlers." Nobody on the bridge visualized the
great berg-studded floe drifting slowly across the ship's
path. The missed messages told a lot.

Above all, the cumulative effect of the messages—
warning after warning, the whole day long—was lost
completely. The result was a complacency, an almost
arrogant casualness, that permeated the bridge.

This complacency is perhaps the most exasperating
feature of the whole affair. Fourth Officer Boxhall did
not even read the one message he saw. Third Officer
Pitman saw the chit marked "ice" above the chart room
table, but it failed to stir his interest—"I only looked at
it casually." Fifth Officer Lowe also looked at the chit
"casually," but once he saw the ship wouldn't reach the
position during *his* watch, he put it out of his mind.
Second Officer Lightoller never even saw the chit when
he came on duty that last Sunday night, "because I did
not look."

Strangest of all was an exchange between Lightoller
and Sixth Officer Moody, who shared the watch from
8:00 to 10:00 P.M. Early on, Lightoller asked Moody
when the ship would be up to the ice. Moody said about
11:00. Working it out for himself, Lightoller decided

the time would really be closer to 9:30. But he never told Moody. Instead, he merely made a mental note of the Sixth Officer's lapse, as though Moody were an errant schoolboy who had made some minor mistake in math, not worth fussing over.

Later Lightoller said he thought that Moody's calculations might have been based on some other ice message that Lightoller himself hadn't seen, but this still doesn't explain his silence. Nor does it help that the collision did not occur until 11:40—well after the time even Moody expected ice. The incident remains a striking illustration of the complacency that seems to have affected the whole bridge.

Yet there was still ample opportunity to avoid disaster. Every officer on the bridge, from Captain Smith to the very junior Moody, knew that sometime before midnight the *Titanic* might encounter ice. It was with this thought in mind that the Captain left the Wideners' party shortly before 9:00 and joined Lightoller on the bridge.

The conversation was oddly laconic. As they peered into a black cloudless night, Smith remarked it was cold. Lightoller: "Yes, it is very cold, sir. In fact, it is only one degree above freezing." He described the precautions he was taking: a warning to the carpenter to watch his fresh water supply . . . another to the engine room to keep an eye on the steam winches.

Smith got back to the weather: "There is not much wind."

"No, it is a flat calm, as a matter of fact."

"A flat calm. Yes, quite flat."

Then, to the ice. Lightoller remarked that it was rather

a pity the breeze didn't keep up while they were going through the danger area. Icebergs were so much easier to spot at night, if the wind stirred up some surf. But they decided that even if the berg "showed a blue side," they would have enough warning. At 9:25 the subject was exhausted and the Captain turned in: "If it becomes at all doubtful, let me know at once. I'll be just inside." Not one word about slowing down. Why was this most obvious of all precautions not even mentioned? The usual answer is that Captain Smith thought the *Titanic* was unsinkable. But even if the ship were unsinkable, the Captain surely didn't want to hit an iceberg.

Actually, he didn't slow down because he was sure that on this brilliantly clear night any iceberg could be spotted in time to avoid it. In reaching that decision, Smith did not feel he was doing anything rash. He was following the practice of all captains on the Atlantic run, except for a few slowpokes like James Clayton Barr of the Cunarder *Caronia,* whose legendary caution at the slightest sign of haze had earned him the derisive nickname "Foggy."

Knuckling under the competitive pressure of keeping schedule, most captains ran at full steam, despite strong evidence that ice was not as easily sighted as generally claimed. Especially noteworthy was the harrowing ordeal of the Guion Liner *Arizona* in November 1879. Like the *Titanic,* she was the largest liner of her day. Eastbound off the Banks of Newfoundland, she raced through a night that was cloudy, but with good visibility. Taking advantage of the calm seas, the passengers gathered in the lounge for a concert.

Suddenly there was a fearful crash, sending everybody sprawling among the palms and violins. The *Arizona* had smashed head on into a giant iceberg, shattering 30 feet of her bow. But the forward bulkhead held; there were no casualties; and two days later she limped into St. John's. In a curious twist of logic, the accident was hailed as an example of the safety of ships, rather than the dangers of ice.

There were other close calls too. In 1907 the North German Lloyd Liner *Kronprinz Wilhelm* dented her bow and scarred her starboard side, brushing a berg in the pre-dawn darkness. In 1909 the immigrant ship *Volturno* barely escaped damage, running through a huge ice field. In 1911 the Anchor Liner *Columbia* struck a berg off Cape Race, driving her bow plates back ten feet. The jar injured several crewmen and broke one passenger's ankle. It was foggy at the time; so perhaps the accident was discounted.

Such incidents were ignored; most captains continued to run at full speed. Always dangerous, the practice became even more so with the vast leap in the size of ships at the turn of the century. It was one thing to dodge an iceberg in the 10,000-ton *Majestic*, Captain Smith's command in 1902, but quite a different matter only ten years later in the 46,000-ton *Titanic*. The momentum of such a huge ship was enormous, and she just couldn't stop suddenly or turn on a dime.

There's no record that the *Titanic* even tested her minimum turning circle during those brief trials in Belfast Lough. Nor did she ever test how long it would take to stop at various speeds, if her engines were reversed. In fact, she never went faster than 18 knots during her trials; her response to commands beyond that point remains a mystery. Once again the question arises: how much did Captain Smith really know about the great vessel under his feet?

Arguably, the practice of maintaining speed might have been a practical necessity in the days before wireless, for who knew where the ice really was? The sightings came from vessels reaching port several days later, and by that time the information was too stale to pinpoint the danger. But Signor Marconi's genius changed everything. The reports reaching the *Titanic* told exactly where the ice could be found, only hours away.

Why couldn't Captain Smith and his officers see the difference? Certainly they knew the importance of wireless in an emergency. The help summoned by the sinking liner *Republic* in 1909 proved that. But no one on the *Titanic's* bridge seemed to appreciate the value of wireless as a constant, continuous navigational aid. Basically, they still thought of it as a novelty—something that lay outside the normal running of the ship. It was a mindset tellingly illustrated by the way the wireless operators were carried on the roster of the crew. Phillips and Bride were not listed with the Deck Department; they came under the Victualling Department—like stewards and pastry chefs.

So the *Titanic* raced on through the starlit night of April 14. At 10 P.M. First Officer Murdoch arrived on the bridge to take over Second Officer Lightoller's watch. His first words: "It's pretty cold."

"Yes, it's freezing," answered Lightoller, and he added that the ship might be up around the ice any time now. The temperature was down to 32°, the water an even colder 31°. A warm bunk was clearly the place to be, and

Lightoller quickly passed on what else the new watch needed to know: the carpenter and engine room had been told to watch their water, keep it from freezing . . . the crow's nest had been warned to keep a sharp lookout for ice, "especially small ice and growlers" . . . the Captain had left word to be called "if it becomes at all doubtful."

Lightoller later denied that the sudden cold had any significance. He pointed out that on the North Atlantic the temperature often took a nose dive without any icebergs in the area. Indeed this was true. The sharp drop in temperature did not necessarily mean ice, but it was also true that it *could* mean ice. It was, in short, one more signal calling for caution. After all, that was the whole point of taking the temperature of the water every two hours.

There's no evidence that either Lightoller or Murdoch saw it that way. The bitter cold and the reported ice remained two separate problems. Lightoller had passed on all the information he could; so now he went off on his final rounds, while Murdoch pondered the empty night.

A few yards aft along the Boat Deck, First Wireless Operator Phillips dug into a stack of outgoing messages. His set had a range of only 400 miles during daylight, and the American traffic had piled up. Now at last he was in touch with Cape Race and was working off the backlog. Some were passenger messages for New York—arrival times, requests for hotel reservations, instructions to business associates. Others were being relayed for ships no longer in direct touch with the land.

At 11 P.M. the steamer *Californian* suddenly broke in: "I say, old man, we're stopped and surrounded by ice." She was so close that her signal almost blasted Phillips's ears off.

"Shut up, shut up," he shot back, "I'm busy. I'm working Cape Race." Then he went back to the outgoing pile—messages like this one relayed to a Los Angeles address from a passenger on the *Amerika:*

> NO SEASICKNESS. ALL WELL.
> NOTIFY ALL INTERESTED. POKER
> BUSINESS GOOD.   AL.

In the crow's nest Lookouts Fleet and Lee peered into the dark. There was little conversation; they were keeping an extra-sharp lookout. At 11:40 Fleet suddenly spotted something even blacker than the night. He banged the crow's-nest bell three times and lifted the phone to the bridge. Three words were enough to explain the trouble: "Iceberg right ahead."

Now it was Murdoch's problem. He put his helm hard astarboard, hoping to "port around" the ice, and at the same time pulled the engine room telegraph to STOP, and then REVERSE ENGINES. But it was too late: 37 seconds later the *Titanic* brushed by the berg with that faint, grinding jar that every student of the disaster knows so well.

The 37 seconds—based on tests later made with the *Olympic*—are significant only for what they reveal about human miscalculations. At 22½ knots the *Titanic* was moving at a rate of 38 feet a second . . . meaning that the berg had been sighted less than 500 yards away. But all the experts agreed that on a clear night like this the ice should have been seen much farther off. Lightoller thought at least a mile or so, and this undoubtedly reflected Captain Smith's opinion, for they both had gone over this very point on the bridge shortly after 9:00. The search immediately began for some extenuating circumstance that could explain the difference.

Suspicion focused first on the lookouts. How good were their eyes? Fleet's had not been tested in five years, and Lee's not since the Boer War. Yet tests after the collision showed both men had sound vision. Nor were they inexperienced. Unlike most lines, White Star used trained, full-time lookouts, who received extra pay for their work.

Next, it was the lookouts' turn to complain. They charged that there were no binoculars in the crow's nest. A pair had been supplied during the trip from Belfast to Southampton, but during a last-minute shake-up of personnel they had been removed and never replaced. After hearing numerous experts on the subject, the British Inquiry decided that it really didn't matter. Binoculars were useful in identifying objects, but not in initially sighting them. That was better done by the naked eye. Here, there was no problem of identification; Fleet knew all too well what he had seen.

Then Lookout Lee came up with a "haze" over the water. He described dramatically how Fleet had said to him, "Well, if we can see through that, we will be lucky." Fleet denied the conversation and said the haze was "nothing to talk about." Lightoller, Boxhall, and Quartermaster Hitchens, who had been at the wheel, all described the night as perfectly clear. In the end, the British

Inquiry wrote off Lee's "haze" as an understandable bit of wishful thinking.

Lightoller himself contributed what became known as the "blue berg" theory. He argued that the iceberg had recently capsized and was showing only the dark side that had previously been under water, making it almost invisible. But this theory did not seem to fit the recollections of the few survivors who actually saw the berg. It was anything but invisible to Quartermaster Rowe, standing on the after bridge. He estimated that it was about 100 feet high, and he initially mistook it for a windjammer gliding along the side of the ship with all sails set.

The only explanation left was "fate." As Lightoller put it, the *Titanic* was the victim of an extraordinary set of circumstances that could only happen once in a hundred years. Normally there would have been no problem, but on this particularly freakish night "everything was against us."

But this explanation implies that Captain Smith didn't know—and couldn't be expected to know—the nature of the night he was up against. But he *did* know. He fully realized that the sea was flat calm, that there was no moon, no wind, no swell. He understood all this and took it into account in deciding not to reduce speed. Under these circumstances the collision quickly loses its supernatural quality and becomes simply a case of miscalculation.

Given the competitive pressures of the North Atlantic run, the chances taken, the lack of experience with ships of such immense size, the haphazard procedures of the wireless room, the casualness of the bridge, and the misassessment of what speed was safe, it's remarkable that the *Titanic* steamed for two hours and ten minutes through ice-infested waters without coming to grief any sooner.

"Everything was against us"? The wonder is that she lasted as long as she did.

CHAPTER VII

The Gash

What did the iceberg really do to the *Titanic,* and could anything have been done to save her? The report of the official British Inquiry found that "the damage extended over a length of about 300 feet," and this is generally taken to mean a continuous gash running from the bow for 300 feet along the starboard side of the ship. Countless illustrators have depicted it in books and magazines—a single, jagged slash, ugly and lethal-looking.

Actually, such a gash would have sunk the *Titanic* in less than an hour. The true nature of the damage may be partly revealed as exploration of the wreck continues over the coming years, but it will often be hard to tell what was done by the iceberg and what was caused by the avalanche of boilers that hurtled down and out of the hull during the *Titanic's* final plunge. Some of the damage may also be buried in the mud and sand where the vessel lies, hidden from the roaming eye of any video camera. Even the most sophisticated equipment will

probably tell us less than a little-known witness at the
British Inquiry, who was nowhere near the *Titanic* that
night, but who knew her far better than any survivor or
future investigator.

Edward Wilding was a naval architect at Harland &
Wolff. His primary concern had been the design of the
Titanic, and he seemed to have at his fingertips every
conceivable dimension of the ship. He knew, for instance, the exact length of each watertight compartment.
Using these figures, he estimated that the gash along the
starboard side must have run some 249 feet—the length
of the first five compartments plus the first two feet of
the sixth.

Estimating the width of the gash was more complicated, but he found some clues in the testimony of various witnesses who had been on the spot. Ten minutes
after the crash, Leading Fireman Fred Barrett saw eight
feet of water in Boiler Room 6, which was five feet above
the keel of the ship. Ten minutes later, Third Officer
Pitman watched bags of registered letters floating
around the mail room, 24 feet above the keel. Another
five minutes and the squash court was awash, 32 feet
above the keel. Fifteen minutes more, and the sea was
flooding into the seamen's quarters on E Deck forward,
48 feet above the keel. Putting the evidence together,
Edward Wilding estimated that 16,000 cubic feet of water had entered the shattered hull in the first 40 minutes.

What size hole would produce this result? Here Wilding's educated guess had to be built on certain basic
assumptions. First, he assumed that the witnesses were
accurate in their estimates of time and the depth of the

water at their particular vantage point. He also assumed that the draft of the *Titanic* would be the same as that of the *Olympic* at the same stage in the voyage. All this granted, he then calculated that the area of damage had to be 12 square feet. Anything else would not fit his timetable.

But this posed a new problem. If the damage was really a continuous gash 249 feet long, then it could only have averaged ¾ of an inch high. Nothing else would work out at 12 square feet. Since this was most unlikely, it followed that the gash was not continuous, but rather a series of separate pokes and stabs as the berg bumped along the side of the *Titanic*. Some of these stabs were great rents like the hole in No. 1 hold, where the berg penetrated 3½ feet inside the ship, ripping the protective casing of the firemen's spiral stairs. Other times the ice barely pierced the hull, like the hole in Boiler Room 5, which spouted a stream as thin as a deck hose. Occasionally, bits of the berg broke off as it brushed by, making the pattern of holes still more irregular.

Whatever the nature of the wound, there was no doubt that it was fatal. It completely flooded the first five compartments, pulling the bow down so far that the water in the fifth compartment eventually slopped over the top of the after bulkhead into the sixth, which in turn overflowed into the seventh, and so on until the ship had to sink.

Later, much was made of the fact that the watertight bulkhead between the fifth and sixth compartments went only as high as E Deck. If this bulkhead had been carried one deck higher, to D Deck, the *Titanic* would not have sunk. This is true, assuming that the only damage to the sixth compartment came from the two-foot gash in Boiler Room 5. This was easily controlled by the pumps.

But this was not the only damage to the sixth compartment. As Edward Wilding pointed out, the gash that ran from Boiler Room 6 into Boiler Room 5 couldn't help but hurt the bulkhead that stood in between. Unlike the gash, this wound was not readily visible to the firemen and engineers, but it was there all the same, and about an hour after the collision the whole bulkhead seems to have given way. From somewhere forward, a great rush of water surged into Boiler Room 5, driving out the men still on duty there.

Nor was that all. There's important, often-overlooked evidence that the next compartment aft, Boiler Room 4, suffered damage entirely independent of the gash. Initially, there was no sign of damage here, but an hour and 40 minutes after the crash, water began seeping over the floor plates from somewhere below. The flow was gradual, but more than the pumps could handle. For a while the firemen toiled on, still shutting down the boilers. The water was up to their knees when the welcome word finally came from the engine room, releasing them from duty. They quickly scrambled up the escape ladders to the temporary safety of the Boat Deck.

It must be emphasized that this water came from below, not above. The flooding of Boiler Room 4 was not part of the process of the forward compartments filling and overflowing into the next compartment aft. Rather, it came from a separate injury to the ship, probably to the double bottom, entirely apart from the familiar gash along the starboard side. In short, the ice did even more mischief than generally thought.

The water in this compartment should also end all theorizing about what might have happened if the bulkheads had been carried one deck higher. With Boiler Room 4 gone, the ship was doomed no matter how high the bulkheads might have been carried. At best, the sinking might have been delayed—perhaps until help came—but the ultimate loss of the *Titanic* was certain.

There's no evidence of damage any farther aft than Boiler Room 4, and this poses an intriguing mystery. If, as the British Inquiry said, the *Titanic*'s bow was just beginning to swing to port when the collision occurred, then the stern would have tended to slue to starboard— toward the ice, rather than away from it. This should have led to some sort of contact with the berg along the whole length of the hull.

What caused the opposite to happen and the stern apparently swing clear of the berg? One explanation might lie in the exchange between Captain Smith and First Officer Murdoch, when the Captain rushed from his quarters onto the bridge immediately after the impact.

"What have we struck?" asked Smith.

"An iceberg, sir," replied Murdoch, "I hard-astarboarded and reversed the engines, and I was going to hard-aport around it, but she was too close. I could not do any more."

Murdoch's explanation has confused many an armchair navigator. It may help to point out that in 1912 a ship's wheel was rigged so that the helmsman turned it to starboard in order to go to port—a holdover from the days when ships were steered by tillers. In 1924 the wheel was re-rigged to cater to the instincts of a generation raised on the automobile, but everyone on the

Titanic's bridge would have been used to the old way.

At least two survivors gave testimony indicating that Murdoch did indeed try to "port around" the berg. Quartermaster Alfred Olliver, coming on the bridge right after the collision, said he definitely heard orders to put the helm hard aport. About the same time Able Seaman Joseph Scarrott, alarmed by the jar, rushed out of the forecastle onto the forward well deck in time to see the berg still passing alongside the ship. The *Titanic* at that moment seemed to be under port helm, her stern gliding away from the ice.

Scarrott undoubtedly reported what he thought he saw, but his account seems highly implausible. It would have been impossible for a ship the size of the *Titanic* to have responded to a change in helm so quickly. A motorboat yes; a 46,000-ton liner, no. Moreover, there's strong evidence that Murdoch never did actually try to carry out his plan. He intended to "port around" the berg, but abandoned the idea when he saw "she was too close." Quartermaster Hitchens, at the helm, testified that the last order he received was "hard-astarboard." Fourth Officer Boxhall, approaching the bridge just before the crash, heard only the same order, followed by the ringing of engine room telegraph bells. Reaching the bridge seconds later, he noted that the telegraph was set at FULL SPEED ASTERN—which made no sense if Murdoch still intended to dodge the ice.

Then why *did* the afterpart of the *Titanic* escape damage? Perhaps the answer lies with the other protagonist in the drama. Much has been said about what the iceberg did to the *Titanic*, but very little about what the *Titanic* did to the iceberg. It is generally pictured as a great natural force, impervious to the assault of mere man, yet we do know that the jar sent chunks of ice tumbling down onto the forward well deck of the ship. Edward Wilding, for one, thought that the same process was going on beneath the surface of the sea as the berg brushed by. If so, it seems reasonable that a large enough chunk may have broken off to end all further contact with the hull.

The first moments after the collision are among the most difficult to sort out. A series of rapidly changing orders jangled from the bridge to the engine room, but none of the surviving witnesses agreed on the exact sequence, the timing, or even the purpose. Greaser Fred Scott testified that immediately after the collision, the engine room telegraph bells rang STOP ENGINES . . . then, 10 or 15 minutes later, SLOW AHEAD . . . another 10 minutes and again, STOP ENGINES . . . then 4 or 5 minutes and SLOW ASTERN . . . 5 more minutes and once again, STOP ENGINES. This time they stopped for good.

Trimmer Patrick Dillon, the only other survivor from the engine room, thought that the signal STOP ENGINES came immediately *before* the crash, that SLOW ASTERN came *before* SLOW AHEAD, and that the time intervals were much shorter—for instance, the ship went SLOW AHEAD for only two minutes, not ten. Neither man remembered the engines being set at FULL SPEED ASTERN, as recalled so clearly by Fourth Officer Boxhall on the bridge.

It is fruitless to turn to the bridge for clarification. Captain Smith, First Officer Murdoch, and Sixth Officer Moody were all lost; Fourth Officer Boxhall was off making a quick inspection; Quartermaster Hitchens was in the wheelhouse unable to see anything; Quartermaster Olliver was running errands most of the time. Olliver does remember the Captain telegraphing HALF SPEED AHEAD sometime during the interval when the *Titanic* lay almost dead in the water.

Many passengers, too, recall the ship starting ahead again, mostly because it seemed so comforting. Second Class passenger Lawrence Beesley, for instance, took a couple of jittery ladies into a bathroom on D Deck and had them touch the tub, where the vibration of the engines was always noticeable. Reassured, the ladies went back to their cabin.

Why the *Titanic* started ahead again, how long and how fast she went, and which direction she took are all intriguing mysteries, important in fixing her correct position when she began calling for help. It has been suggested that Captain Smith was making for the light of another ship on the horizon, but this seems unlikely for two reasons. First, there's no evidence that such a light had yet been sighted; and second, Captain Smith had no reason yet to suspect that his ship had been seriously injured. In fact, Fourth Officer Boxhall's first, quick inspection (as far down and forward in the passengers' quarters as he could go) brought the good news that he could find no damage at all.

The bad news came soon enough—from the carpenter, from Holds 1, 2, and 3, from the firemen's quarters, from the mail room, from Boiler Rooms 5 and 6. If Smith still had any hope, it was dispelled by the arrival of Thomas Andrews on the bridge. As Managing Director of Harland & Wolff, Andrews knew the ship more intimately than anyone else on board. He gave the *Titanic* "from an hour to an hour and a half."

Could anything have been done to save her? It's a favorite subject for letter-writers, and over the years suggestions have ranged from stuffing the gash with bedding to a headlong run for the light that glimmered most of the night on the horizon.

No amount of bedding could have stemmed the torrent pouring into the *Titanic*, but the possibility of using collision mats was at least considered by the British Inquiry. After a brief discussion, Edward Wilding rejected the idea on two grounds: first, it was impossible to fix the exact location of the various holes to be plugged; and second, 50 to 60 men would have been needed to rig collision mats, and they couldn't possibly be organized and deployed before it was too late to do any good.

Steaming for the light can be ruled out too, because it was not sighted soon enough. The light was first seen a few minutes after midnight, and by that time the funnels were blowing off great clouds of steam—a sure sign that the boilers had shut down for good. Even if the light had been sighted sooner, it's highly doubtful that the *Titanic*'s shattered hull could have stood the strain of the dash.

Others contend that the watertight doors should have been reopened once the extent of the damage was known. This would have allowed the water to spread gradually throughout the hull, and the ship would have settled on an even keel. This way, the *Titanic* would have taken longer to sink than she actually took going down by the head. The British Inquiry agreed, but did not press the point. The damage was so overwhelming, it made little difference whether the doors were left open or shut.

Actually, there seemed to be only one moment when the *Titanic* really might have been saved, and that came at the very start of the crisis, when Lookout Fleet reported the iceberg to the bridge. If First Officer Murdoch had steamed right at the berg instead of trying to miss it, he might have saved the ship. There would have been a fearful crash—passengers and crew in the first 100 feet would have been killed by the impact—but the *Titanic* would have remained afloat.

It would have been like the *Arizona*, 33 years earlier. Tumbling out on deck, her passengers found her crumpled bow pressed against the ice. Fearing the end, they clung to each other in tears. Yet it was not the end, and when they finally realized that the *Arizona*'s collision bulkhead would hold, they joined in a prayer of thanks and sang the hymn "Praise God from Whom All Blessings Flow."

The *Titanic* was not the *Arizona*. She hit the berg a glancing blow, not head on; but Murdoch could not be blamed for trying to miss it. He did what he had been trained to do—what any prudent officer would do—in the same circumstances. His great misfortune was that, in his own succinct words, "she was too close."

Now that it had happened, there was only one course left open for Captain Smith. It was almost exactly midnight—the 12:00 to 4:00 watch was just coming on deck in a last display of normal shipboard routine—when he gave the order to take to the boats.

CHAPTER VIII

"I Was Very Soft the Day I Signed That"

The decision to take to the boats brought Captain Smith face-to-face with a painful mathematical fact: there were lifeboats enough for only 1,178 of the 2,201 people on board the *Titanic*. Even if every boat got away filled to capacity, 1,023 individuals would be left behind with no chance of escape.

It could have been worse. The *Titanic* was certified to carry 3,547 passengers and crew, but due to the slack season and uncertainties of travel during the coal strike, she was only two-thirds full. Also, the Board of Trade regulations required her to carry boats for only 962 persons, but the White Star Line liked little flourishes and threw in space for an extra 216. In a "worst case" situation the *Titanic* might lawfully have gone to sea with lifeboats for only 27% of her passengers and crew.

Responsibility for this state of affairs went back to a regulatory body called the Board of Trade, which set the safety standards for British ships. The *Titanic* came under the Board's regulations governing vessels of "10,000 tons and upwards," the maximum category at the time the rules were issued in 1894. Since then the size and capacity of ships had increased dramatically—the *Titanic* was nearly four times as large as any vessel of the 90's—but the lifeboat requirements remained the same.

At the time of the disaster it was generally felt that the lag was due to a somnolent Board of Trade, full of sleepy figureheads and bureaucrats who failed to keep up to date. Actually, the problem was more complicated than that. The Board's requirements were inadequate not only for the new breed of giants like the *Titanic,* but for ordinary vessels of the type they were written for. Of 39 British liners over 10,000 tons, 33 did not provide lifeboats for everybody, yet fully complied with the law. Some, like the *Megantic, Zeeland,* and *Saxonia*—all under 20,000 tons—had boats for less than 50% of those who might be aboard. The Cunarder *Carmania* could take care of only 29%.

Nor was the problem limited to vessels coming under Britain's Board of Trade. The ships of other nations, too, rarely carried enough boats for all on board. The German liner *Amerika* could accommodate only 55%; the American liner *St. Louis,* 54%. Based on a random sampling of ships on the North Atlantic run, only the French liner *La Provence* came anywhere near providing boats for all. She could provide space for 82% of her passengers and crew.

In brief, ships of all nationalities—and all sizes—fell short, yet sailed the North Atlantic with official blessing.

Surely, all the regulators everywhere couldn't have been asleep. There had to be a better explanation.

There was. The problem was not somnolence; it was subservience. The members of the Board of Trade itself knew little about ships or safety at sea. They were mostly decorative luminaries like the Archbishop of Canterbury. On nautical matters they deferred to the professional staff of the Board's Marine Department. But these men were bureaucrats—better at carrying out policy than making it. When it came to such questions as whether ships should provide lifeboats for all on board, these men deferred to the Department's Merchant Shipping Advisory Committee. This group was dominated by the shipowners themselves, and they were only too happy to make policy. They knew exactly where they stood, and they did not want boats for all.

In the luxury trade, "boats for all" meant less room on the upper decks for the suites, the games and sports, the verandahs and palm courts, and the glass-enclosed observation lounges that lured the wealthy travelers from the competition. On the *Titanic*, for instance, it would sacrifice that vast play area amidships and instead clutter the Boat Deck with (of all things) boats.

In steerage, the other place where there was big money to be made, "boats for all" would be even more costly. In calculating the number of lifeboats needed, the Board of Trade used a simple rule of thumb: each person took up ten cubic feet of space. Hence 1,134 steerage passengers—the number the *Titanic* was certified to carry—would require 11,340 cubic feet of space. This translated into 19 lifeboats required for steerage alone . . . or nearly 60 boats, counting everybody. Almost any owner would prefer to use most of this space in some revenue-producing way—if he could persuade himself that the boats weren't really necessary.

This proved easy to do. The new superliners could easily ride out the storms and heavy seas that sometimes engulfed steamers of the past. Increased compartmentalization seemed safer, since no one could imagine anything worse than being rammed at the point where two compartments joined. The development of wireless should end the days when ships simply disappeared. In the future, lifeboats would only be used to ferry passengers and crew to the gathering fleet of rescue ships, and nobody needed "boats for all" to do that.

It didn't take long for the owners to convince themselves that the concept was positively dangerous. Piling all that gear on the upper decks would make a vessel top-heavy, or "tender," as nautical men put it. Also, the top decks would be so congested that the crew would have no room to work, if it did indeed become necessary to abandon ship.

Finally, there was the weather. The stormy Atlantic was no place to float the 50 to 60 lifeboats required for a ship the size of the *Titanic,* if "boats for all" was the rule. Nineteen times out of 20, estimated White Star's general manager Harold Sanderson, the boats could not be lowered safely. Once afloat, passengers would be subject to additional dangers as they bobbed around waiting for rescue. "They could avoid all this by drowning at once," dryly observed the magazine *Fairplay,* when Sanderson persisted in his views even after the disaster.

The utter speciousness of the owners' arguments became clear within days of the sinking. All the obstacles to "boats for all" suddenly vanished. "The lifeboat capacity of these steamers will be ample to provide for every person aboard," the Hamburg-American Line assured the public. Despite Mr. Sanderson's views, White Star fell in step with the rest. When the *Olympic* sailed from New York, April 25, the line's announcement emphasized that she would have "boat and life raft capacity for every person on board, including both passengers and crew."

But that came later. Until the *Titanic,* the public seemed perfectly willing to accept the owners' arguments. Like air travelers today, a liner's passengers understood that if the ship went down, they might well go with it. As White Star's Sanderson put it, "There are certain risks connected with going to sea which it is impossible to eliminate."

One man saw through this nonsense—and was in a perfect position to do something about it. The Right Honourable Alexander M. Carlisle was Managing Director of Harland & Wolff in 1909, while the *Olympic* and *Titanic* were on the stocks. A big, hulking man, he ran the shipyard with tyrannical discipline, and was accustomed to getting his way. Nor did it hurt that he was the brother-in-law of Lord Pirrie, Harland & Wolff's Chairman.

For some time Carlisle had been uneasy about the small number of lifeboats to be carried by the two new giants. There were only 16, which met the 1894 regulations, but seemed too few for the size of the ships. Since the contract with White Star clearly left such matters to Harland & Wolff, he asked the Welin Davit Company in Sweden to design for him new davits that would hold up to 64 boats, although he felt that 48 would be enough.

Later, much would be made of Carlisle's unsuccessful efforts to achieve his goal. First intimations came three days after the disaster, when the newspaper *Daily Mail* carried an interview with him on April 18, 1912. Asked whether he felt the Board of Trade requirement on lifeboats was sufficient, Carlisle replied, "No, I do not think it is sufficient for big ships, and I never did. As ships grew bigger, I was always in favor of increasing the lifeboat accommodation." He went on to explain that, feeling as he did, he had fitted the *Olympic* and *Titanic* with davits that could handle "over 40 boats," but he didn't say why the boats themselves were never included.

The closest he came was a curious observation later in the interview: "If any ships had been fitted with the full number of boats I proposed, it would no doubt have set up an invidious situation with respect to the steamers of all lines now trading in the North Atlantic. It would have drawn attention." In other words, enough lifeboats on one or two liners might start people worrying about the lack of boats on all the others. This ostrichlike approach was overlooked in the general applause that greeted at least one man in the shipping business who appreciated lifeboats.

Seventy-one years later Carlisle again became the hero who had fought in vain for more boats. In 1983 a British television documentary, "The *Titanic*—A Question of Murder," described how Carlisle "conducted a lengthy campaign to increase by two or even three times the number of lifeboats carried by the great liner." According to the script, he "argued" and "recommended" in vain, opposed by an intransigent Bruce Ismay, head of the White Star Line.

Such a dramatic conflict is the stuff that great TV shows are made of, but in real life this clash never happened. Carlisle did indeed think the *Titanic* should have had more lifeboats—he wanted 48 altogether—but he never told Bruce Ismay so. He merely proposed special *davits* that could carry additional boats, pointing out that this would save money if the Board of Trade later tightened its regulations. His point was economy, not safety.

When the British Inquiry asked why he didn't recommend more boats as well as the special davits, Carlisle replied that there were limits to what he could, with all propriety, propose to White Star. It was not his position to make such an expensive recommendation.

When asked why Harland & Woff's cost-plus contract with White Star didn't allow the yard to act on its own, Carlisle patiently explained that there were limits here too. True, White Star boasted that the agreement gave the builders free rein to turn out the best-equipped ship regardless of expense, yet it wasn't quite that simple. Whatever the contract said, there was a tacit understanding that Harland & Wolff mustn't go too far. If they loaded the *Olympic* and *Titanic* with lifeboats, that would leave White Star in an embarrassing position with the rest of its fleet. They might be expected to give those ships enough boats too—and that could get very expensive.

Feeling unable either to recommend or act on his own, Carlisle merely showed the plans of the ship to Bruce Ismay, leaving Ismay to discover for himself that the Boat Deck provided for 48 boats, if White Star thought that desirable. It was almost like a valentine being slipped under the door by a faint-hearted suitor.

Not surprisingly, Ismay never approved the idea. In fact, he later claimed that he never even saw the plan for the lifeboat arrangements. Since the subject of boats took up only five or ten minutes in each of two all-day conferences, he may have been telling the truth.

Certainly, Carlisle didn't push the point. The roaring lion—so accustomed to getting his own way at the shipyard—turned into a pussycat when it came to dealing with the client.

Yet "Big Alec" still had a chance. If he was reluctant to press his views on a client, he had another opportunity under entirely different circumstances in May 1911. The occasion was a meeting of the Board of Trade's Merchant Shipping Advisory Committee, called to reconsider the whole question of lifeboats. By now Carlisle had retired from Harland & Wolff, but was added to the Committee because of his special expertise on the subject.

Behind closed doors, he argued strongly for more boats on the great new liners. Not surprisingly, the Committee—dominated as always by the owners—turned a deaf ear to his advice. Then the unexpected twist: Carlisle not only remained silent at the rebuff, but signed a set of recommendations that actually reduced the number of lifeboats required on a ship like the *Titanic*.

"Was that your view?" an incredulous Lord Mersey later asked at the Inquiry.

"It was not," replied Carlisle.

"Why on earth did you sign it?"

"I don't know why I did. I am not generally soft."

"Well, I should not have thought so," broke in the

Attorney General, apparently trying to ease the strain. "But I must say," continued Carlisle, "I was very soft the day I signed that."

So much for the hero. By the time the *Titanic* sailed, April 10 the following year, Carlisle was no longer directly concerned. He said he didn't even know how many boats she was carrying.

Captain Smith knew. At midnight, April 14–15, he was all too well aware that his ship had only 16 wooden boats in the davits—the same number originally planned before Alexander Carlisle played his hesitant role. In addition, there were four "Englehardt collapsibles," semirafts with wooden bottoms and canvas sides. They were not in davits, but stowed flat on deck, upside down with the sides folded in. If they were ever needed, the idea was to assemble them and fit them into the davits of boats already lowered. This must have been considered a remote possibility, for two of them were stowed on the roof of the officers' quarters, with no way to get them down to the Boat Deck.

Now it was up to Captain Smith to make the best of this small fleet, with an untried crew, uninformed passengers, and a ship that had never held a proper boat drill.

LOST — SAVED

Category	Lost	Saved
FIRST CLASS PASSENGERS	118 MEN / 4 WOMEN / 0 CHILDREN	57 MEN / 140 WOMEN / 6 CHILDREN
SECOND CLASS PASSENGERS	154 MEN / 13 WOMEN / 0 CHILDREN	14 MEN / 80 WOMEN / 24 CHILDREN
THIRD CLASS PASSENGERS	387 MEN / 89 WOMEN / 52 CHILDREN	75 MEN / 76 WOMEN / 27 CHILDREN
TOTAL PASSENGERS	659 MEN / 106 WOMEN / 52 CHILDREN	146 MEN / 296 WOMEN / 57 CHILDREN
TOTAL CREW	670 MEN / 3 WOMEN	192 MEN / 20 WOMEN
TOTAL PASSENGERS AND CREW	1329 MEN / 109 WOMEN / 52 CHILDREN	338 MEN / 316 WOMEN / 57 CHILDREN

Source: Report, British Inquiry

CHAPTER IX

What Happened to the Goodwins?

At midnight, April 14–15, the shortage of lifeboats on the *Titanic* was academic; the question was, who would get to use them. The White Star Line always claimed that the only rule was, "Women and children first"; there was absolutely no distinction, the line insisted, between First, Second, and Third Class passengers.

Both the American and British investigations agreed, and Mr. W. D. Harbinson, who officially represented Third Class at the British Inquiry, emphatically concurred:

> I wish to say distinctly that no evidence has been given in the course of this case that would substantiate a charge that any attempt was made to keep back the third class passengers. There is not an atom or a tittle of evidence upon which any such allegation could be based. . . .

Yet there remained those uncomfortable statistics: 53% of First and Second Class passengers saved, but only 25% of Third Class. . . . 94% of First and Second Class women and children saved, but only 42% of those in Third Class. In First Class just one child was lost—little Lorraine Allison, whose family decided to stick together—while in Third Class, 52 out of 79 children were lost—about the same percentage as First Class men.

The White Star Line was full of explanations: the Third Class passengers were more reluctant to leave the ship. . . . They didn't want to part with their luggage. . . . It was hard to get them up from their quarters. At the British Inquiry one member of the crew after another assured the Court that there was no discrimination whatsoever—but not a single Third Class passenger was called as a witness.

The Court accepted all of White Star's explanations, and seemed especially impressed by the point that many of the steerage passengers were foreign and couldn't understand the crew's instructions.

How, then, to explain the loss of the entire Goodwin family—father, mother, and six children? There was no "language barrier" here; they were from London. Nor is there any reason to suppose they were unwilling to leave the ship, or especially reluctant to part with their luggage.

Frederick Goodwin was no ordinary, uneducated emigrant. He was a 40-year-old electrical engineer who lived with his wife, Augusta, and their six children in a small but neat row house in Fulham. As the family grew, Mr. Goodwin began looking around for new opportunities. His brother Thomas had already left the old country and settled in Niagara Falls, New York; so when Thomas wrote of an opening at the big power station there, Frederick jumped at the chance.

He got rid of the house in Fulham, paused briefly at Marcham, and booked passage for himself and family on one of the more modest steamers operating out of Southampton. These were the days before new employers paid relocation costs, and since the Goodwins had little in the way of savings, they would be traveling Third Class.

Then came the lucky break. Due to the coal strike, their sailing was canceled, and they were transferred to the new, glamorous *Titanic*. They were still in Third Class, but on the *Titanic* that was as good as First Class on most of the older, smaller liners. The Goodwins probably occupied two of the four-berth cabins at the very stern of the ship, which White Star reserved for single women and families traveling together. Single men were quartered in the bow, but during the day all Third Class passengers mingled on deck and in the various public rooms. They could go anywhere they liked, as long as they didn't cross the various barriers and gates that barred access to Second and First Class space.

On White Star ships, Third Class was encouraged to retire by 10 P.M., and the Goodwins were undoubtedly in bed when that faint, grinding jar shook the *Titanic* at 11:40 on the night of April 14. Whether they were awakened by the jar no one knows, but they were certainly up shortly after midnight, when the Third Class bedroom stewards went through the long white corridors, banging on doors and telling everybody to put on their life belts.

Pouring into the hallways, the passengers tended to congregate at the foot of the main Third Class stairway on E Deck. Here they waited for instructions from above, while the bedroom stewards adjusted the life belt straps and assured them that there was no need to worry. It's easy to imagine the Goodwins, nervous but faintly amused by the odd sight of each other in their bulky life belts: Frederick, with arms folded as in the family photograph . . . Augusta, with her old-fashioned upswept hairdo . . . Lillie, 16, her dark hair hanging casually over her shoulders . . . Charles, 14, alert, erect, every inch the oldest brother . . . then William, Jessie, Harold, and Sydney, all under 12, good soldiers but uncomprehending.

Word gradually spread that the *Titanic* had hit an iceberg, but the first truly alarming development came when the single men, driven from the bow by the rising water, swarmed aft and joined the crowd milling around the stairs. Many of these men carried satchels and bundles, sopping wet from the seawater that had swirled into their quarters.

And so the crowd waited—restless, complaining, but certainly not rebellious. Their only clue to the condition of the ship was the definite forward tilt of the linoleum beneath their feet. The lights still burned brightly, and buried as they were on E Deck, they couldn't see that the *Titanic*'s lifeboats were now dropping to the sea and rowing off into the night.

Shortly before 1 A.M., the long-awaited instructions came: "Pass the women and children up to the Boat Deck." The order was by no means easy to carry out. Here and there, wives refused to leave their husbands,

Belfast, Ireland, May 31, 1911. Lubricated by 23 tons of tallow, train oil, and soft soap, the new White Star Liner *Titanic* slides down the ways, destined to become the largest ship in the world. All Belfast turned out for the show. Curiously, there was no christening ceremony. As one shipyard worker explained, "They just builds 'er and shoves 'er in." COURTESY HARLAND & WOLFF

Surpassing the Greatest Buildings and Memorials of Earth

The Largest and Finest Steamers in the World ☆ "OLYMPIC" AND "TITANIC"
White Star Line's New Leviathans ☆ 882½ Feet Long   92½ Feet Broad   45,000 Tons

White Star publicity experts did their best to convey the immense size of the new vessel. Here the *Titanic* and her sister ship *Olympic* are compared to eight of the most famous structures on the face of the earth.   AUTHOR'S COLLECTION

The *Titanic* was as luxurious as she was big. The 28 special staterooms on B Deck, designed to win the "millionaire trade," were the most opulent on the Atlantic. This picture shows the paneled elegance of B-63.   COURTESY HARLAND & WOLFF

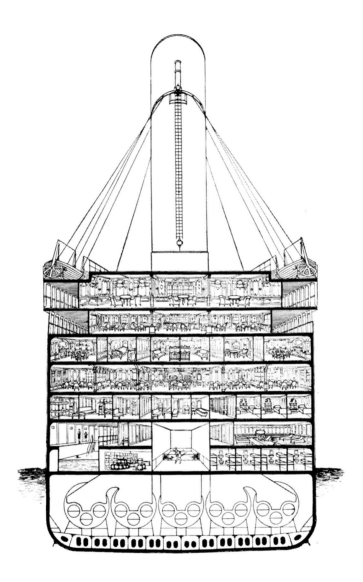

The transverse view was a favorite promotional device. It conveyed both size and luxury. Carried away by his enthusiasm, the artist here has substituted a tennis court, complete with net, for the more modest squash court actually provided. AUTHOR'S COLLECTION

The only time the *Titanic* ever dressed ship: Good Friday, April 5, 1912. Taken at Southampton five days before sailing for New York. AUTHOR'S COLLECTION

Captain Smith (right) with Purser McElroy, photographed on the Boat Deck, starboard side forward, just outside the officers' quarters. PAUL POPPER

Sailing Day, April 10. Second Class passenger Charles Whilems, leaving on a business trip to New York, poses with his daughter and a friend alongside the *Titanic*'s massive fourth funnel. COURTESY THE LATE FRANK GOLDSMITH

The *Titanic* narrowly escapes collision as she leaves Southampton. The suction caused by the forward motion of her huge hull tore the smaller liner *New York* from her moorings. A serious accident was prevented only by quick action in stopping the *Titanic*'s engines. BROWN BROTHERS

Queenstown, April 11. Captain Smith looks down from the bridge for a last picture. Taken from the tender that has just brought out 113 Irish emigrants—mostly young people looking for fresh opportunities in the New World. PAUL POPPER

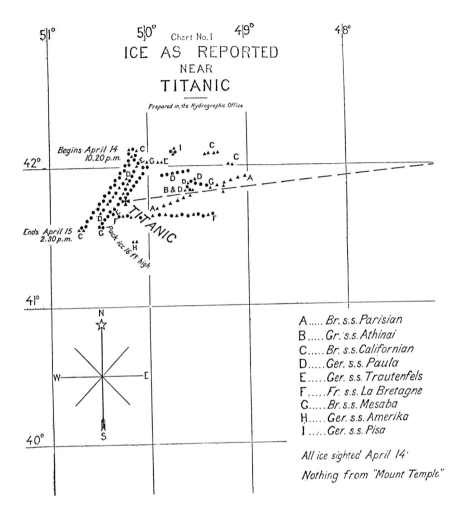

ICE AS REPORTED
NEAR
TITANIC

Prepared in the Hydrographic Office

A.....Br. s.s. Parisian
B.....Gr. s.s. Athinai
C.....Br. s.s. Californian
D.....Ger. s.s. Paula
E.....Ger. s.s. Trautenfels
F.....Fr. s.s. La Bretagne
G.....Br. s.s. Mesaba
H.....Ger. s.s. Amerika
I.....Ger. s.s. Pisa

All ice sighted April 14·
Nothing from "Mount Temple"

Sunday, April 14. The air crackled with wireless warnings of ice ahead. Pieced together, they indicated an enormous ice field, studded with bergs, drifting southward across the Atlantic steamship lanes. The *Titanic* acknowledged receipt of six such messages, but nobody on the bridge seems to have grasped their collective significance. This reconstruction of the danger zone was plotted after the disaster by the U.S. Navy Hydrographic Office. U.S. SENATE, DOCUMENT NO. 726, 62ND CONG., 2ND SESS.

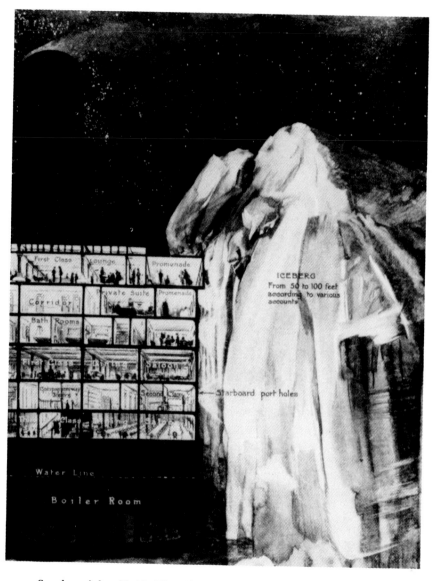

Sunday night, 11:40. The *Titanic* scraped an iceberg, ripping her hull as depicted here by the magazine *Sphere*. By midnight Captain Smith knew the worst and ordered all passengers on deck with life belts. AUTHOR'S COLLECTION

Climbing the grand staircase to the Boat Deck, Mrs. Helen Churchill Candee (upper left) encountered a shipboard friend, Edward A. Kent (upper right), and persuaded him to take for safekeeping her most cherished possession, an ivory and gold miniature (lower right) of her mother. When Kent's body was later recovered, the miniature was still in his jacket pocket and was returned safely to Mrs. Candee. COURTESY MRS. ALAN BARKER; AUTHOR'S COLLECTION

The rule was "women and children first"—but not always in Third Class. The entire Goodwin family were among those lost. In this group portrait, they are, from the left: William, 11; Frederick, 40; Charles, 14; Harold, 9; Lillian, 16; Augusta, 43; and Jessie, 10. Sidney, 6, is missing from the picture. AUTHOR'S COLLECTION

Although the *Titanic* had far too few lifeboats, ironically many of them rowed away less than half full. The empty seats in this boat drawing alongside the rescue ship *Carpathia* could have held all the Goodwins plus 20 more. AUTHOR'S COLLECTION

The HEROIC MUSICIANS OF THE TITANIC
who died at their posts like men ~ April 15th 1912

G. KRINS Violin.

W. HARTLEY
BANDMASTER.

R. BRICOUX Cello.

W. T. BRAILEY Piano.

P. C. TAYLOR, Piano.

J. W. WOODWARD Cello.

Nearer, my God, to Thee.

Or if on joyful wing cleaving the sky,
Sun, moon and stars forgot, upwards I fly,
Still all my song shall be,
Nearer, my GOD, to Thee, nearer to Thee.

"Nature might stand up,
And say to all the world,
This was a man."
—Julius Cæsar

J. F. C. CLARKE Bass.

J. L. HUME Violin.

Playing to the end, the entire band was lost. The members' heroism became an instant legend, but the White Star Line left them completely unprovided for. This broadside was sold by the British Musicians' Union to raise money for their families. COURTESY MUSICIANS' UNION

The Cunard Liner *Carpathia* (above) caught the *Titanic*'s wireless call for help and raced 58 miles through ice-strewn waters to the rescue. Among the 705 saved was Second Officer Lightoller, who went down with the ship and miraculously lived to tell the story. He is pictured at the right on the trip back to New York, standing between Captain Rostron and another officer of the *Carpathia*.

AUTHOR'S COLLECTION

As the *Carpathia* was picking up the last *Titanic* lifeboat, the Leyland Liner *Californian* arrived on the scene. She was left to continue searching the area while the Cunarder headed back to New York. Photographed from the *Carpathia* by passenger Louis M. Ogden. AUTHOR'S COLLECTION

Captain Stanley Lord of the *Californian* (seated, left) with three of his officers. During the night she had lain nearby, stopped by the ice. The men on her bridge saw rockets and suspected a ship in trouble, but nothing was done until morning. Then the wireless operator, off-duty asleep, was finally awakened, and the *Californian* learned what had happened. MIRRORPIC

The official British Inquiry lasted 36 days, but for many, the high point came on the eleventh day with the testimony of Sir Cosmo and Lady Duff Gordon. Their lifeboat, capacity 40 persons, left the *Titanic* with only 12, and Sir Cosmo had been accused of bribing the crew not to take more. Titillated by the possibility of scandal in high places, London society packed the hearing room. The *Illustrated London News* staff artist catches the scene as Sir Cosmo cleared himself of all charges. UPPER LEFT, ILN PICTURE LIBRARY; UPPER RIGHT AND BOTTOM, LONDON ELECTROTYPE AGENCY

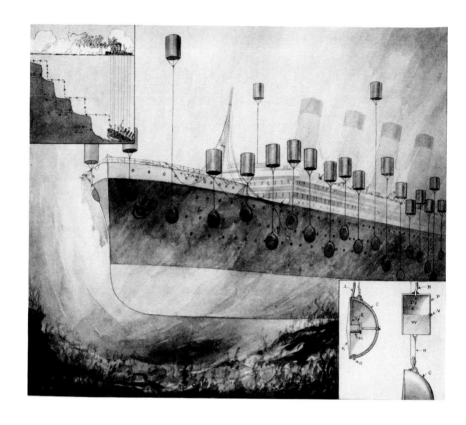

The *Titanic* was gone but not forgotten. Over the next 70 years countless plans were put forward to find and raise her. Most made use of the latest technology, like this early plan featuring electromagnets. Even the most fanciful fell far short of the intricate combination of wide-scanning sonar, video cameras, banks of strobe lights, and ultrasensitive film (ASA 200,000) that actually did locate the *Titanic* in 1985. AUTHOR'S COLLECTION children clung to their fathers, and some of the women still refused to believe there was any serious danger. A few even went back to their bunks.

Somehow Steward John E. Hart managed to collect a group of 30, and leading the way, he escorted them up the stairway to C Deck, across the open well deck, by the Second Class library, and into First Class space. Then on forward to the C Deck foyer, and finally up the grand staircase to the Boat Deck. The route seems to have been set in advance, for all the barriers were down, and here and there other stewards were posted to nudge them along.

It was now 1:10, and Boat 8 was about to leave. Hart handed over his charges to the men at the falls and headed back to steerage for another group.

By the time he reached the Third Class stairs again, matters had taken an ugly turn. The male passengers were now demanding to go up to the Boat Deck too, and it was all the stewards could do to hold them back. Finally, another convoy was organized, and Hart again set out. This time he had about 25 in tow and reached the Boat Deck around 1:35. As far as he could see, there were no boats left except No. 15, still in the davits but ready to be lowered.

Not a moment to lose. He bundled his people into the boat and made a lightning assessment: the *Titanic* was finished . . . no time to go back for one more group. With a nod from the officer standing by the davits, Hart too jumped into the boat.

In all, he had brought up some 55 women and children—nearly half the total number saved—but the Goodwins weren't among them. Possibly the family refused to be parted. Possibly they remained below, waiting in vain for one more party to be escorted topside. Possibly they tired of the long wait, struck off on their own, but never made it to the Boat Deck until too late.

It's difficult even to speculate, not because of any set policy to hold back Third Class, but because there was no policy at all. Some gates were open; some were closed. Some passengers were assisted; others were stopped; others were left to shift for themselves.

Berk Pickard, a 32-year-old leather worker from London, found a door to Second Class wide open, easily made his way to an early boat. Kathy Gilnagh, a 15-year-old colleen had no such luck. When she and two friends tried to pass through the gate to Second Class from the after well deck, they found it closed and guarded. It took some powerful persuasion by Jim Farrell, a strapping lad from Kathy's home county, to persuade the guard to open it long enough for the girls to slip through.

All the way forward, Daniel Buckley, another young Irishman, joined a group trying to force their way up the ladder leading from the well deck to First Class. Here, too, the gate was closed and guarded, and after a brief scuffle, the seaman on duty locked it as well. Undaunted, the leader of Buckley's group stormed up the ladder again and smashed the gate open—lock and all— as the seaman fled.

Olaus Abelseth and four friends, all from Norway, waited for what seemed an eternity in the after well deck. The barriers leading to Second Class were closed, and they whiled away the time watching the more agile steerage passengers climb up a crane, crawl out on the boom, and drop safely into First Class, the ultimate goal of everyone. At last an officer opened the barrier and called for the women and children to go to the Boat Deck. A little later he called for "Everybody." Abelseth and the rest of the men surged up, only to find that all the boats were gone.

And so it went: no set policy, but incident piled on incident, all combining to make a mockery of Mr. Harbinson's assurances that there was "not an atom or a tittle of evidence" to substantiate a charge that any attempt was made to keep back the Third Class passengers. Even Steward Hart's testimony, heavily relied on by the White Star Line, showed clearly that the men in steerage were held back and that the women had what amounted to an hour's handicap in the race for the boats.

Oddly enough, while the Third Class passengers were having such a hard time, many of the lifeboats were leaving the *Titanic* only half-filled. Considering that at best there was room for only half those on board the ship, it seems incredible that the space available—good for 1,178 people—was occupied by only 705. There was room for another 473—far more than enough for all the women and children lost. Why wasn't it used?

At the bottom of the trouble was the lack of organization that characterized the whole night. The *Titanic* had never held a boat drill, and few of the crew had any experience in handling the davits. They had boat assignments, but these had only been posted the day after leaving Queenstown. Few had bothered to look up their stations. The manning of the boats was hopelessly haphazard: No. 6 had a crew of only two; No. 3 had 15.

The passengers had no boat assignments at all. They

simply milled around the decks waiting for someone to
tell them what to do, but there were no clear lines of
authority. Later it was said that First Officer Murdoch
was in charge on the starboard side, Second Officer
Lightoller on the port. But Lightoller never got aft of
the first four boats, nor had anything to do with the first
boat, No. 2. The junior officers didn't seem to have any
assignments, and nobody even remembered to wake up
Fifth Officer Lowe. Finally aroused by some unusual
noise on the Boat Deck, he looked out and saw passengers standing around in life belts.

There was no consistency in loading the boats. To
Lightoller, "Women and children first" meant women
and children only, even if that meant not filling a boat.
Murdoch, on the other hand, put in men when there
were no women. On the *Titanic,* a man's life could de-
pend on which side of the Boat Deck he happened to
step out on.

Then there was the recurring problem of class distinction. At least some of the crew, and passengers too,
believed that the boats were reserved for the class where
they were located. When two Second Class ladies asked
an officer if they could pass to the forward boats in First
Class space, passenger Lawrence Beesley heard the officer reply, "No, madam, your boats are down on your
deck."

This basic lack of organization was especially apparent in the actual loading of the boats. No. 4 was the first
one ready, and Captain Smith ordered Lightoller to fill
it from the Promenade Deck, feeling that it would be
easier and safer than the exposed Boat Deck for the
women and children. The order was passed on to the

passengers already waiting on the Boat Deck, and they obediently trooped below. Watching the scene, First Class passenger Hugh Woolner seems to have been the first person to realize that this wasn't such a good idea. "Haven't you forgotten, sir," he politely asked Smith, "that all those glass windows are closed?"

"By God, you are right!" exclaimed the old captain. "Call those people back." He had apparently forgotten that the forward end of the *Titanic*'s Promenade Deck was enclosed, confusing her with her sister ship the *Olympic*, where the deck was open for its full length.

So everyone was ordered up again, and the women and children quietly climbed back to the Boat Deck. But by this time Boat 4 had been lowered to the Promenade Deck as originally ordered, and Lightoller decided it would be easier to open the windows than to haul the boat back up. A couple of seamen were sent to do this, and the women and children were ordered back down. "Tell us where to go and we will follow," exclaimed an exasperated Mrs. Thayer. "You ordered us up here and now you are taking us back."

No firm procedure was ever followed. In the end, some of the boats were loaded from the Boat Deck, others from the Promenade Deck—meaning that the passengers were often not where the boats were.

Mrs. Thayer's outburst was prompted by irritation, not fear. For the first hour, few of the *Titanic*'s passengers took the collision very seriously—which is another reason why the early boats, at least, didn't contain more people. They far preferred the warmth and comfort of the brightly lit ship to the prospect of spending a dark, cold night bobbing about the Atlantic in a rowboat. When

the first boat to be loaded, No. 7, was swung out and
First Officer Murdoch called for passengers, only a
trickle responded. He finally lowered the boat at 12:45
with just 28 persons aboard.

Murdoch now moved on to No. 5, the next boat aft,
and again called for passengers. Hovering nearby was a
small party of six, traveling together: Mr. and Mrs.
Richard Beckwith, Mr. and Mrs. E. N. Kimball, Miss
Helen Newsom, and Karl H. Behr. They were reluctant
to go, even after Bruce Ismay urged them to get into the
boat. Finally, Mrs. Beckwith edged forward and asked
Ismay if her whole party, men and women, could go
together. "Of course, madam," Ismay replied, "every
one of you."

So they all climbed in, and at 12:55, No. 5 was lowered
with just 41 people . . . meaning there was still room for
another 24. As the boat jerked down toward the sea 70
feet below, Karl Behr wondered whether this precau-
tion he was taking was worth the risk. Any idea that the
Titanic might sink was "preposterous."

Not everyone was that confident. There was, for instance, "our coterie" in the smoking room. Interrupted
by the jar, they soon resumed their bridge game, but it
wasn't as jolly as before. After a hand or two, Hugh
Woolner and Bjornstrom Steffanson excused themselves
and went below to check on Mrs. Candee. They found
her standing outside her stateroom door wondering
what had happened, puzzled but all right. Steffanson
apparently went back to the smoking room, but by now
the ship had stopped, and Woolner invited Mrs. Candee
for a walk "to see how things are going."

They had spent an enchanting afternoon together exploring the vessel, and now they were doing it all over again—only this time things were different. The Boat Deck was dark and bitter cold; the funnels were blowing off steam with a deafening roar; the *Titanic* had a pronounced list to starboard. They nervously cracked a few jokes; touched on their personal troubles, and even talked of life and death. They drifted into the lounge, where they had enjoyed such a cozy tea that afternoon. Now it was empty, but a cheerful young man suddenly appeared and handed Mrs. Candee a small chunk of ice. It was so cold she dropped it, and Woolner found himself at first chafing and then caressing her hand.

They moved to the Promenade Deck and heard the sailors above beginning to swing out the boats. Wandering by the entrance to the grand staircase, they saw passengers streaming up, all wearing life belts. "Is this orders?" Woolner asked a man by the door. "Orders," the man briefly replied.

Back down to Mrs. Candee's stateroom; Woolner found her life belt and tied it on her. Then he hurried off to get his own, promising to meet her in a few minutes topside.

As she started up the stairs, Edward A. Kent—another charter member of the coterie—dashed up. On impulse, she handed him a small ivory miniature of her mother, asking him to keep it for her. He had doubts about his own safety, but slipped it into his pocket. It was still there when his body was picked up a week later.

Woolner and Steffanson reappeared, and together they hurried Mrs. Candee into Boat 6, the first lifeboat lowered on the port side. Of the coterie, Colonel Gracie seems to have been the busiest. He had already offered his services to four other "unprotected ladies," and now he was doing his best to see them all into the boats. It was after 1:00 before he began searching for Mrs. Candee. He finally ran into Kent, who assured him that she was safely off the ship.

By now there was no lack of people willing to leave the *Titanic*, but a new problem arose. The officers in charge of launching the boats were afraid to put too many passengers in them for fear they might buckle and pitch everyone into the sea. Actually, there was no danger of this. Harland & Wolff had designed all the boats on the *Olympic* and *Titanic* to be lowered with their full complement of people. In a test on May 9, 1911, the shipyard even loaded one of the *Olympic*'s boats with weights corresponding to 65 persons, then raised and lowered it six times without any sign of strain.

Neither Captain Smith nor his officers seem to have been aware of the test. Harland & Wolff never told them that the boats could be lowered fully loaded; the builders simply assumed they knew this as "a matter of general knowledge." If they ever knew, nobody remembered it that night. Boat 6 rowed off with a maximum of 28 people; Boat 8 with 39; Boat 2 with 26.

Acting on his own, Lightoller decided he might get more people into the boats by utilizing the portside lower deck gangway. He sent six seamen down to open the doors, and ordered the boats, once afloat, to row down to the opening and receive additional passengers. It didn't work. The doors were never opened; the men sent down were never seen again. They were probably trapped by some sudden inflow of water before they could get the job done.

There was apparently a similar plan for boats on the starboard side. Lawrence Beesley recalled hearing an officer—Murdoch, he thought—calling down to the crew of No. 13, "Lower away, and when afloat, row around to the gangway and wait for further orders." Captain Smith was also calling on the boats to stay within hailing distance.

Some did . . . for a while. But the sight of that great hulk, lights ablaze, sagging into the ocean proved too frightening. She was clearly doomed now, and there was talk of suction and a huge wave that would swamp any boats that remained too close. One by one they crept away into the night.

On the *Titanic* herself, the mood had changed to desperation. By 1:15 the water was lapping at the letters of her name on the bow. Drunkenly, she staggered from a slight list to starboard to a heavy list to port. The downward tilt of the deck grew steeper.

Time was running out. The officers in charge of loading the boats no longer hesitated to fill them: No. 11 went off with 70; No. 14 with 63; No. 15 with 70.

But haste could also be costly. It probably explains the worst case of the night of a boat leaving the *Titanic* with too few people. Technically, No. 1 was called an "emergency boat"—smaller than a regular lifeboat, manned by a specially trained crew, and ready for instant launching in such untoward situations as a man overboard. It was the first boat on the starboard side, just aft of the bridge.

Since No. 1 was always kept swung out, the crew did not bother with it when they first came on deck to clear the boats. Instead, they started with No. 3 and worked their way aft. The crowd on the Boat Deck followed along, and by the time First Officer Murdoch turned his attention to No. 1, the only passengers in the vicinity were a rather haughty English couple, Sir Cosmo and Lady Duff Gordon, and Miss L. M. Francatelli, who was Lady Duff Gordon's secretary. There seems no clear reason why they didn't go aft with the mob; perhaps it just wasn't their way of doing things.

When the boat was ready for launching, Murdoch called for women and children, but none appeared. Lady Duff Gordon had already made up her mind that she would never leave her husband, and Miss Francatelli wouldn't go alone. Finally, Sir Cosmo stepped up and asked if all three couldn't enter the boat. Murdoch replied, "Yes, I wish you would." They climbed in, as he again called for women and children. This time two American businessmen came up, and Murdoch put them in too.

Hundreds of women must have been still on the Boat Deck, but Murdoch apparently felt there was no time to search for them. His one idea seems to have been to get the boat away. The ship was sinking fast, and he needed the empty davits for the two starboard collapsibles. He plucked two seamen and five stokers from members of the crew standing by, put Lookout George Symons in charge, and told him to lay off 200 yards, ready to come back when summoned. At 1:10, Boat 1, capacity 40 persons, dropped down to the sea with just 12 people aboard, only 5 of them passengers.

There would have been less need to hurry, if the *Titanic*'s crew had been better trained in loading and lowering the lifeboats. Two hours should have been enough to do the job properly. But Captain Smith's casual approach to the whole matter of boat drill now took its toll. His custom on the *Olympic*—carried over to the *Titanic*—was merely to test two lifeboats once a voyage, always while the ship was tied up at dock. A picked crew of experienced seamen—usually the same team every time—would lower the boats to the water, then raise them up again. The stewards participated only occasionally, and the firemen not at all. As a result, there were not enough trained hands, and on the night of April 14, the boats could not be lowered simultaneously, but had to be launched one at a time.

Boat 4 offers a prime example of what could happen. This was the boat that Second Officer Lightoller had been unable to load from the Promenade Deck because all the windows were closed. They were soon opened, but by that time Lightoller and his team of "old hands" had moved on to Boat 6 . . . then to Boat 8 . . . and finally to Collapsible D, which was still lashed to the Boat Deck. More than an hour passed before he got a chance to break off and finish launching No. 4. Meanwhile the women waiting to enter the boat simply cooled their heels.

By now it was nearly 2:00, and the water was only ten feet below the Promenade Deck. The women were hurriedly rounded up and passed through the windows into the boat. The pace was so frantic that Lightoller was bathed in sweat, despite the 32° temperature. Colonel Gracie and some of the other First Class men pitched in to help—experience no longer mattered. In the rush to get the boat off, 20 places were left unfilled.

Even the last boat lowered, Collapsible D, was

launched with plenty of room in the bow. As it dropped by the open end of the Promenade Deck, Hugh Woolner and Bjornstrom Steffanson were standing there and noticed the empty space. They decided to jump for it as the water washed onto the deck and over their evening slippers. This was a dangerous thing to do, for boats hanging in davits are notoriously tippy, but they got away with it, and Collapsible D pulled away with 44 of its 47 places filled.

There remained Collapsibles A and B, stowed on the roof of the officers' quarters on either side of the forward funnel. These boats, too, were never fully utilized, but here the explanation was not haste or complacency. It was a case of poor design. It's hard to imagine what Harland & Wolff had in mind when they put two boats in such an inaccessible spot. There was absolutely no mechanism for getting them down to the Boat Deck, where they then had to be fitted into the empty davits used by the two emergency boats.

Nevertheless, the crew did their best. Murdoch led a small group trying to free Collapsible A on the starboard side, while Lightoller's men struggled with Collapsible B on the port side. With enormous effort the two boats were wrestled to the edge of the roof, and oars were placed against the wall of the officers' quarters to slide them down to the Boat Deck. A handful of passengers quietly looked on, trying to calculate their chances. Should they wait here on the slim hope of a place in these two boats, or should they head aft toward the momentary safety of the poop deck?

Colonel Gracie and Clinch Smith decided to head aft, but suddenly their way was blocked by a great mass of steerage passengers—hundreds of them—surging up the companionway and deck ladders from somewhere below. Who they were, or where they had been until now, remains a mystery. Had they been restrained until this last desperate moment? Had they been waiting to be escorted to the Boat Deck, when time simply ran out? No one will ever know, for all were soon engulfed by the water now sweeping up the deck.

There were women as well as men in this crowd, and it offers our best clue to what happened to the Goodwin family. Sticking together, they probably reached the Boat Deck too late for a chance at the boats. Now, somewhere in this nameless, faceless mass of human beings, Frederick and Augusta Goodwin stood with their six children, quietly prepared to meet the end.

CHAPTER X

Shots in the Dark

At least the *Titanic* was spared the horror of a panic. The crew did not battle the passengers for the lifeboats, as they did when the French liner *La Bourgogne* went down in 1898. No officer "stole" a boat, as happened when the Collins Liner *Arctic* sank in 1854.

With few exceptions, the passengers behaved admirably, and the crew did their duty—often at a fearful price. The statistics tell the story: the Captain, Chief Officer, and First Officer—all lost; the engineers—all lost; the pursers and officers of the Victualling Department—all lost; the eight bandsmen—all lost; the five bellboys—all lost.

Fearing there might be trouble, the officers loading the boats were armed with pistols, but in more than 2,000 pages of testimony at the hearings, there is only one thoroughly documented case in which a gun was fired. As Boat 14 was being lowered, a group of steerage passengers tried to jump in, and Fifth Officer Lowe fired several shots along the side of the ship to keep them out.

There also seems to have been some gunfire during the loading of Collapsible C—the last boat lowered on the starboard side forward—which takes on added interest since it was the boat that took off Bruce Ismay, head of the White Star Line. Ismay never mentioned any disorder at the hearings, nor did Quartermaster George Thomas Rowe or Pantryman Albert Pearcey, the only other persons in the boat to testify. Yet Hugh Woolner was quite specific on the point, both in a letter written on the *Carpathia* and later in his testimony at the Senate investigation.

According to Woolner, he and Steffanson had just finished helping Lightoller load Collapsible D, all the way forward on the port side, when they heard a commotion across the deck on the starboard side. They crossed over just in time to see First Officer Murdoch fire his pistol twice in the air, trying to stop a rush on "a collapsible"—which could only have been Collapsible C. Woolner and Steffanson helped restore order, then saw the boat safely away.

In an account privately published for his family and friends in 1940, First Class passenger Jack Thayer partially corroborated Woolner's story. . . .

There was some disturbance in loading the last two forward starboard boats. A large crowd of men was pressing to get into them. No women were around as far as I could see. I saw Ismay, who had been assisting in the loading of the last boat, push his way into it. It was really every man for himself. . . . Purser H. W. McElroy, as brave and as fine a man as ever lived, was standing up in the next to last boat, loading it. Two men, I think they were dining room stewards, dropped into the boat from the deck above. As they jumped, he fired twice in the air. I do not believe they were hit, but they were quickly thrown out.

There are, of course, nagging discrepancies between Woolner's and Thayer's accounts. Woolner thought First Officer Murdoch fired the shots; Thayer thought Purser McElroy did. Woolner thought it was the last boat; Thayer thought it was the next-to-last. But survivors often saw things differently in the dimly lit confusion of the *Titanic's* Boat Deck; and overriding any discrepancies, it seems to me, is the basic similarity: both Woolner and Thayer, responsible witnesses, independently recalled an officer firing twice into the air to stop a rush on one of the last boats on the starboard side forward.

In both Woolner's and Thayer's accounts it should be emphasized that the shots were fired into the air, not at anybody. Through the years there have also been stories of actual shootings, but serious students have largely written them off as the concoctions of a sensationalist press that stopped at nothing for dramatic effect. I have always gone along with this reasoning.

It was, then, quite a surprise some years ago to run across a personal letter from a survivor—not just another wild newspaper story—describing an actual shooting in the last minutes on the Boat Deck. The letter was from Third Class passenger Eugene Daly to his sister in Ireland. It is undated, but was clearly written right after the disaster, since it appeared in the London *Daily Telegraph* on May 4, 1912. Describing the scene, Daly wrote:

At the first cabin [deck] when a boat was being lowered an officer pointed a revolver and said if any
man tried to get in, he would shoot him on the spot.
I saw the officer shoot two men dead because they
tried to get in the boat. Afterwards there was another shot, and I saw the officer himself lying on the
deck. They told me he shot himself, but I did not
see him. I was up to my knees in the water at the
time. Every one was rushing around, and there were
no more boats. I then dived overboard.

Daly ended up among the survivors who reached one
of the collapsibles that floated off the ship; so he was
at least in a position to see. Still, it was only one letter.
To be taken seriously, it needed some sort of confirma-
tion.

That came in 1981 with the publishing of *The Titanic,
the Psychic and the Sea* by Rustie Brown. In the course of
her research, Mrs. Brown ran across an unpublished
letter from First Class passenger George Rheims to his
wife in France. It is dated April 19, 1912, the day after
the *Carpathia* reached New York with the *Titanic*'s survivors. Rheims was one of the few who jumped near the
end and ultimately reached Collapsible A; he, too, was
in a position to see. Originally written in French, here is
a translation of the pertinent part of his letter:

While the last boat was leaving, I saw an officer with
a revolver fire a shot and kill a man who was trying
to climb into it. As there remained nothing more
for him to do, the officer told us, "Gentlemen, each
man for himself, Good-bye." He gave a military salute and then fired a bullet into his head. That's
what I call a man!!!

These strikingly similar accounts come from completely independent sources. There's no reason to suppose that Eugene Daly and George Rheims were ever in touch. Both were writing a private letter to an intimate member of the family, not an account for the press. Both were writing immediately after the event, not years later when fantasy might have taken over. They had absolutely no reason to fabricate, but every reason to be telling the truth as far as they saw it.

Supposing such an incident really happened, what boat was involved? The guiding clue is in Daly's letter, where he writes that he had no chance to see the officer's suicide because "I was up to my knees in the water at the time." This means that by now the bridge must have dipped under, and the sea was swirling along the Boat Deck. All the boats had been launched except Collapsibles A and B, which had been dropped down to the Boat Deck from the roof of the officers' quarters. On the port side, Collapsible B landed upside down and could only be floated off as a raft. Only Collapsible A on the starboard side could still be launched properly, and members of the crew were desperately trying to hook it up to the davits when the sea came rolling along the deck. One of these men was Steward Edward Brown, whose testimony is our best source on Collapsible A. His account fits well with Daly's letter—he even describes the water washing around his legs. He does not mention any shooting, but concedes there was a great "scramble" to get into the boat. All in all, it seems most likely that Daly was writing about Collapsible A.

Who was the officer involved? Could it have been Purser McElroy? Jack Thayer recalled McElroy firing two shots to stop a rush on one of the forward starboard boats, but Thayer did not think it was the last boat. Apart from that, the officers of the Victualling Department were basically "housekeepers." They were not likely to be in charge of loading and lowering lifeboats, nor would they have the authority to declare "Each man for himself," as Rheims noted. Lightoller in his memoirs recalled saying good-bye to the pursers and doctors, who were standing off to one side of the Boat Deck. He specifically praised their quiet courage for staying out of the way while the deck force launched the last boats.

A far more likely candidate would be one of the three lost officers of the Deck Department. Sixth Officer Moody was on the scene; he was in charge of the party on the roof of the officers' quarters that cut Collapsible A free. On the other hand, once back on the Boat Deck, he would have come under First Officer Murdoch, who was trying to attach the collapsible to the falls. He then wouldn't have had the authority to give the order "Each man for himself."

First Officer Murdoch was in exactly the right spot, working on the collapsible. Moreover, he had been in charge of the bridge at the time of the crash and had given the orders that failed to save the ship. If his thoughts turned to suicide, it was at least understandable. Yet Lightoller and those who knew Murdoch felt he was the last person to take his own life. When last seen, just as Lightoller dove into the sea, Murdoch was still working on the falls.

That leaves Chief Officer Wilde, who is the enigma of the night. None of the survivors had much to say about him. He was new to the ship, and Lightoller's feathers were clearly ruffled at being bumped down a notch to make room for Wilde as "Chief." But silence and our lack of knowledge are not evidence; so in the end there's no more reason to suppose Wilde was the officer seen by Daly and Rheims than anyone else.

The whole incident can't be verified, yet can't be dismissed. It was not just one more lurid tale appearing in the yellow press; it was witnessed and independently described by two separate firsthand sources. It must be taken seriously, but beyond that, it remains a mystery.

CHAPTER XI

The Sound of Music

The last moments of the *Titanic* are full of mysteries—none more intriguing than those surrounding the ship's band. We know they played, but little else. Where they played, how long they played, and what they played remain matters for speculation.

All eight musicians were lost; so there are no firsthand accounts. We can only piece the story together from bits of evidence. The search is made more difficult by a host of legends that have cropped up, and by the fact that few of the *Titanic*'s survivors seem to have been blessed with a very good musical ear.

The whole problem is further complicated by the fact that there were two distinct musical units on the *Titanic,* not just a single eight-piece orchestra, as is generally assumed. First, there was a quintet led by violinist Wallace Hartley and used for routine ship's business— teatime and after-dinner concerts, Sunday service and the like. There was no brass or drums. Vernon and

Irene Castle had introduced the foxtrot, but it hadn't reached the White Star Line yet.

In addition to this basic orchestra, the *Titanic* had something very special: a trio of violin, cello, and piano that played exclusively in the Reception Room outside the À la Carte Restaurant and Café Parisien. This was all part of White Star's effort to plant a little corner of Paris in the heart of a great British liner, and appropriately the trio included a French cellist and a Belgian violinist to add to the Continental flavoring.

These two orchestras had completely separate musical libraries. They had their own arrangements, and they did not normally mix. It is likely (but not certain) that on the night of the collision they played together for the first time. Hence whatever they played had to be relatively simple and easy to handle without sheet music—the current hits and old numbers that the men knew by heart.

Where did they play? Apparently they initially took their stand in the First Class lounge on A Deck around 12:15 A.M. Dressed in their regular uniforms with the green facings, they looked as though it was a perfectly normal occasion. Jack Thayer remembered them playing to a restless crowd milling in and out of the room, not paying much attention.

Later, the band moved up to the Boat Deck level of the grand staircase. Here they were in the mainstream of the passengers heading from their staterooms to the boats. There was a small piano on the port side of the foyer, and it was put to good use.

Near the end, they moved out onto the Boat Deck itself, but still remained near the entrance to the grand staircase. By now the interior of the ship was nearly deserted and if their music was to do any good, they had to be where people could hear them.

How long did they play? Legend has them carrying on with the water practically up to their knees, but by then the slant of the deck would have been so steep, no one could have stood. At the other extreme, Colonel Gracie, on board to the last, said that the band stopped playing about half an hour before the ship sank. He added that he himself saw the musicians lay down their instruments. Curiously, Gracie did not mention this in his authoritative study *The Truth about the Titanic,* but he went into some detail in a talk he gave at the University Club in Washington on November 23, 1912. This was less than two weeks before he died; so it is presumably his last word on the subject.

Gracie's recollection seems confirmed by First Class passenger A. H. Barkworth, also there to the end, who recalled: "I do not wish to detract from the bravery of anybody, but I might mention that when I first came on deck the band was playing a waltz. The next time I passed where the band had been stationed, the members had thrown down their instruments, and were not to be seen."

Barkworth was a stolid Yorkshireman, not given to fantasy. He and Gracie undoubtedly told what they saw, but nothing varies more wildly than estimates of time the night the *Titanic* went down. Other witnesses, equally reliable, remember the band playing almost to the final plunge.

Harold Bride recalls their music while he was on the roof of the officers' quarters struggling to free Collapsible B. Greaser Thomas Ranger heard them when he came up from turning off 45 fans to find all the boats gone. But perhaps the musicians' best epitaph comes from the testimony of Steward Edward Brown at the British Inquiry. When asked how long he heard the band play, Brown replied, "I do not remember hearing them stop."

What were they playing? All agree that the band featured light, cheerful music—ragtime, waltzes, and the comic songs that were then so popular in the London music halls. Survivors specifically recalled Irving Berlin's "Alexander's Ragtime Band" and a pretty English melody called "In the Shadows," the big London hit of 1911. Colonel Gracie couldn't remember the name of any tune, but he was sure the beat was lively to the end. Nevertheless, the *Carpathia* had no sooner reached New York than the story spread that the band went down playing "Nearer, My God, to Thee." The idea was so appealing that it instantly became part of the *Titanic* saga—as imperishable as the enduring love of the Strauses and the courage of the engineers who kept the lights burning to the final plunge.

Yet doubts persist. In the first place, the whole point of the band playing was to keep the passengers' spirits up, and light music seems best suited to that. As Colonel Gracie observed, "If 'Nearer, My God, to Thee' was one of the selections, I assuredly would have noticed it and regarded it as a tactless warning of immediate death, and more likely to create a panic that our special efforts were directed towards avoiding. . . ."

Moreover, no one up close remembered it. For instance, Mrs. A. A. Dick of Calgary, Alberta, vividly recalled seeing the musicians lined up on deck playing "Nearer, My God, to Thee" . . . yet she was in Boat 3, at least a quarter-mile away. On the other hand, passengers Peter Daly and Dick Williams—both on board to the last—agreed with Colonel Gracie: the band played only light, cheerful music.

Finally, we must face the hymnologists. They point out that both British and American survivors recalled "Nearer, My God, to Thee," but ordinarily the hymn is played to entirely different music on the two sides of the Atlantic. In America the setting is normally Lowell Mason's haunting tune "Bethany"; but in Britain the standard Episcopal setting is J. B. Dykes's "Horbury," while the Methodists prefer Sir Arthur Sullivan's "Propior Deo." Unless the band played all three versions (an absurdity), more than half of those who remembered the hymn must have been mistaken.

Sunday service on British liners of the period was normally Church of England, which suggests that Dykes's "Horbury" was used, but to balance that, Bandmaster Hartley had a strong Methodist background. In his hometown, Colne, his father served as choirmaster at the local Methodist church for 30 years and invariably used Sullivan's "Propior Deo." Hartley himself favored this setting, according to a fellow musician who had played with him on another ship. His friends and relatives firmly believed that this was the version played on the *Titanic,* and in fact, the opening bars are carved on the monument over his grave.

The controversy over "Nearer, My God, to Thee" had barely begun when *The New York Times* introduced a brand-new candidate for the band's final number. Based on an exclusive interview with Second Wireless Operator Harold Bride appearing April 19, the morning after the *Carpathia* reached New York, the paper announced on April 21 that the musicians went down playing the Episcopal hymn "Autumn."

The story included an illustration reproducing several lines of the music, and also quoted three stanzas. The first line ran "God of mercy and compassion, look with pity on my pain," and even more appropriate were two lines in the third stanza:

> Hold me up in mighty waters;
> Keep my eyes on things above.

The hymn completely fitted the occasion, and Bride was the perfect authority. He was no distant observer; he was on the Boat Deck to the last. As a wireless operator, he was trained to be meticulously accurate. So "Autumn" it was, both in *A Night to Remember* and in accounts by other writers attempting to get below the surface and discover what really happened.

Then once again, the hymnologists. This time they pointed out that "Autumn" is the name of a hymn tune, and that in both Britain and America hymns are customarily known by their first line, not by the name of the music that provides the setting. Hence we refer to "Onward, Christian Soldiers," not its tune, "Saint Gertrude," and a choir sings "O God, Our Help in Ages Past," not its tune, "Saint Ann." The same goes for "Autumn." If Harold Bride meant a hymn, he would have referred to it by the opening line of some hymn that used this piece of music as a setting.

Even then it would not have been "God of Mercy and Compassion," for there is no Episcopal hymn that begins that way. "Autumn" *was* an alternate setting for the Episcopal hymn "Guide Me, O Thou Great Jehovah," but it seems to have been rarely used and was dropped from the hymnal after 1916.

The hymnologists' case against "Autumn" came through in driblets, and it wasn't until research began on this book that it became clear how convincing it was. The arguments are neatly summarized by Jessica M. Kerr in her article "A Hymn to Remember," appearing in the January 1976 issue of the magazine *The Hymn.*

What, then, was Bride referring to when he mentioned "Autumn"? The most likely answer is contained in a series of letters written to me in 1957 by Fred G. Vallance of Detroit, Michigan. Mr. Vallance was bandleader of the Cunard Liner *Laconia* at the time of the *Titanic* and was writing from the point of view of a shipboard musician. He pointed out that whatever the band played, it had to be something they all knew by heart—something that could be played in the dark, on a sloping deck, and without the benefit of sheet music. The hymn tune "Autumn" did not remotely meet these requirements, but a currently popular waltz, "Songe d'Automne," did.

"Songe d'Automne," moreover, was generally known simply as "Autumn." Composed by Archibald Joyce, it was never very popular in America, but was a major hit in London in 1912. Played at roller-skating rinks, cafés, and the like, Harold Bride would probably have known it, and he might well have assumed that his American interviewers understood what he meant.

Certainly Bride never referred to "Autumn" as a hymn

in his original interview of April 19. He specifically mentioned the tune three different times, but always casually, like a popular song that needed no further explanation. For instance:

> From aft came the tunes of the band. It was a ragtime tune, I don't know what. Then there was "Autumn." Phillips ran aft, and that was the last I ever saw of him. . . .

Nor did *The New York Times* ever check back with Bride on its article two days later, unveiling "Autumn" as the hymn the band played at the end. The story was clearly based on the original interview, without futher amplification.

It's interesting to note that the British press never accepted the idea that the band went down playing any hymn called "Autumn." The *Daily Telegraph* carried the April 19 interview with Bride, but identified "Autumn" as a "ragtime air." This it certainly was not, but the description does indicate that the editors never thought Bride meant a hymn.

Nor did seafaring people think so at the time. According to Vallance, the general opinion among ship musicians was that the *Titanic*'s band played "Songe d'Automne" at least part of the time, and he himself was told this by more than one survivor. Once when he was playing it, a ship's steward (apparently from the *Titanic*) came up and admonished him that it was "unlucky."

Fred Vallance presented his case in 1957, but its true significance wasn't appreciated until research began on this book. The hymnologists had to demolish "Autumn" first. With that out of the way, his theory becomes the most plausible explanation of what really happened.

But it is not carved in stone. There is always the possibility of some totally unexpected twist to the story. For instance, it is conceivable (though not at all likely) that the Café Parisien trio never joined forces with Wallace Hartley's quintet, but continued to play as a separate group, ending with some hymn in another part of the ship. Then there is the question of what pianists Percy Taylor and Theodore Brailey were doing at the end, for it seems most unlikely that anyone dragged a piano out onto the Boat Deck.

Whatever they played, they achieved immortality. The bravery of these men, trying to bring hope and comfort to others without a thought to their own safety, captured the public's imagination all over the world. Editorials, speeches, sermons, and reams of worshipful poetry celebrated the deed, and letters of condolence poured into the homes of the bereaved.

Tucked in with the tributes received by the family of violinist Jock Hume, was a letter to his father that sounded a strangely jarring note. Dated April 30, 1912— just two weeks after the tragedy—it contained no words of sympathy, just a short, crisp reminder:

Dear Sir:

We shall be obliged if you will remit to us the sum of 5s. 4d., which is owing to us as per enclosed statement. We shall also be obliged if you will settle the enclosed uniform account.

Yours faithfully,
C. W. & F. N. Black

The "enclosed uniform account" included such items as a lyre lapel insignia (2 shillings) and sewing White Star buttons on a tunic (1 shilling). Altogether, Hume's account added up to a grand total of 14s. 7d.—or about $3.50 in American money.

C. W. and F. N. Black, who so diligently pursued their $3.50, were Jock Hume's agents, and any entertainer or writer today who complains about his agent would do well to ponder the situation in 1912. He might find things are not so bad after all.

Until 1912 the various steamship lines dealt directly with their musicians, signing them up as members of the crew like stewards, firemen, and ordinary seamen. The pay was union scale, which worked out at £6 10s. a month, plus a monthly uniform allowance of 10s.

Then the Blacks entered the picture. An enterprising talent agency based in Liverpool, they promised the steamship companies a simpler and cheaper way to good music. One after another the companies signed contracts, giving the Blacks the exclusive right to supply bands to their vessels. The musicians still signed the ship's articles for a token shilling a month (putting them clearly under the captain's authority), but they were now really working for the Blacks, and could get no jobs except through the Blacks.

Since the musicians worked for the Blacks or not at all, they had to take what the Blacks were willing to pay them—which turned out to be a sharp cut in salary. Instead of a basic pay of £6 10s., they now got only £4. Instead of a uniform allowance of 10s. a month, they now got nothing at all. The terms of employment were also hard: if the steamship company objected to any musician, the Blacks had the right to remove the man without any investigation or explanation.

The Amalgamated Musicians Union protested without success. Only some of the bandsmen belonged, and in any case, these were not the times for strong union action.

Finally, early in March 1912, a delegation from the union waited upon Bruce Ismay. As Managing Director of the White Star Line, Ismay was a mover and shaker in the British shipping industry, and maybe he could be persuaded to do something. The great *Olympic* was about to sail from Southampton, and the delegation pointed out that her five-man band was being paid at less than union scale, supplemented only by the monthly shilling that White Star paid to make them officially members of the crew.

If the delegation expected to melt Ismay's heart, they didn't know their man. He replied that if the union objected to White Star carrying its bandsmen as members of the crew at a shilling a month, the company would carry them as passengers.

Sure enough, when the *Olympic* reached New York on March 20, her five musicians were listed as Second Class passengers. All had regular tickets, and all had to appear before the immigration officials in the usual way. As a crowning irony in view of the reason for this masquerade, all had to produce $50 in cash to show that they were not destitute.

The masquerade continued when the *Titanic* sailed. She, of course, had not only the standard five-man band, but the special trio added for the Café Parisien. Hence there were now eight extra names on the Second Class passenger list. Otherwise nothing had changed: the musicians still had the same cramped quarters on E Deck (next to the potato washer), and certainly none of the "perks" of passengers. When they played that last night, they played as disciplined members of the ship's crew, not as a group of talented passenger-volunteers.

It was natural, then, for the musicians' families to turn first to the White Star Line for financial benefits under the Workmen's Compensation Act. Sorry, said White Star, the bandsmen were Second Class passengers and not covered by the Act. The Line suggested that the families contact C. W. and F. N. Black, the real employers.

Sorry, said the Blacks. The problem wasn't their responsibility. They carried insurance to cover such matters, and any claims should be laid at the insurer's door.

Sorry, said the insurance company, the bandsmen were not workmen as covered by the policy. They were independent contractors, using the Blacks as a booking agency, and the insurance company was under no liability.

Months passed while White Star, the Blacks, and the insurer tossed this hot potato back and forth. Finally, in exasperation the families took the Blacks to court. The judge was sympathetic, but that was all. The bandsmen, he decided, were not the employees of anybody. They were passengers in the case of the White Star Line, and independent contractors in the case of the Blacks and the insurers.

With the legalities settled, the musicians' union made a final appeal to White Star's sense of moral responsibility: "Three families lost their only sons—three young men ranging from 21 to 24 years of age, cut off in the prime of their life while performing an act of heroism that stirred the whole world to its depths. Surely there is something for the White Star Company to consider over and above the mere terms of an Act of Parliament." It did no good.

In the end, the day was saved by the *"Titanic* Relief Fund," an umbrella organization that was set up to manage the charitable contributions that poured in from all over the world. On January 2, 1913 the Fund announced that it would treat the musicians as though they were members of the crew. This opened the door at last to adequate benefits. Welcome news, but no thanks to the White Star Line. To the end it maintained, as far as I can determine, that the musicians were no more than Second Class passengers.

While this shabby little business was unfolding behind the scenes, front-stage the drama of the band's heroism continued. On May 18 there occurred one of those great public funerals, dripping with melancholy pageantry, that the Victorians and Edwardians did so well. Bandmaster Wallace Hartley's body had been retrieved from the ice-strewn waters off Newfoundland, and now he was coming home to his final rest.

Seven bands played as his rosewood casket, borne shoulder-high, was carried through the winding streets of Colne, Hartley's birthplace in the hills of Lancashire. Aldermen, councillors, ambulance men, police, boys' brigades, and musicians from all over England fell in behind—the procession was a half-mile long. Thousands lined the route; most wore black or white, but occasionally there were mill girls in their drab shawls and miners in their blue overalls. All business had stopped for the day. At the steep hillside cemetery, as the casket was lowered into the grave, a dozen Boy Scouts raised their bugles and sounded "The Last Post." The notes echoed off the neighboring hills, drowning out the squabbling and petty maneuvers for that day at least.

CHAPTER XII

"She's Gone"

The climactic moment of the night came just before 2:20 A.M. The *Titanic*'s stern rose high into the air; the lights went out; and she stood nearly perpendicular to the water, silhouetted against the star-filled sky. She hung there at least a minute, while everything movable broke loose and thundered down through the hull. Then, leaning back slightly, she slid beneath the sea. It was almost like a benediction, Second Officer Lightoller recalled, as the men clinging to overturned Collapsible B breathed the two words, "She's gone."

Lightoller was sure that the *Titanic* went down intact. So was Third Officer Pitman, who watched from Boat 5. Colonel Gracie and Lawrence Beesley, the two survivors who wrote the most authoritative contemporary accounts, both agreed. All in all, a formidable array of experts, and through the years their view became accepted gospel. To question it amounted to heresy.

So it was all the more surprising to find, when the

Titanic was located 73 years later, that the whole stern was missing. Had it broken away during the final plunge, or when the ship hit the ocean floor? The pattern of the debris indicates that the fracture most likely happened as the ship started for the bottom. If so, the whole affair shows once again the danger of relying too much on experts. They are not always right. Here, moreover, there was good reason to question their opinion from the start. After all, Beesley was a mile away in Boat 13; Pitman was at least 400 yards off in Boat 5; and Gracie didn't see the final plunge at all—he was under water fighting for his life. Lightoller did have a swimmer's-eye view, but much of the time he, too, was under water or trying to climb onto overturned Collapsible B. From the collapsible, 250 feet of the *Titanic*'s hull towering over him could easily have looked like an unbroken wall stretching up to infinity.

In contrast, there were other survivors—often with a far better vantage point—who saw things quite differently. In fact, of the 20 witnesses who described the final plunge at the American and British investigations, 16 firmly declared that the *Titanic* either split in two or at least was breaking up as she went under. There is, moreover, a remarkable similarity about what they saw. . . .

- Quartermaster Bright, in Collapsible D, last boat to leave the ship and 100–150 yards away. Ship broke in two; after part briefly righted itself, then plunged down.

- Greaser Thomas Ranger in Boat 4, last regular lifeboat to leave, and 50–100 yards away. Forward end seemed to break off; after part came back on an even keel, then turned up and went down steadily.

- Mrs. Arthur Ryerson, also in Boat 4: *Titanic* suddenly began sinking rapidly. Took a plunge toward the bow; then two forward funnels seemed to lean; then she seemed to break in half as if cut with a knife, and as bow went under, the lights went out. Stern stood up for several minutes, then that too plunged down.

- Able Seaman F. O. Evans, Boat 10, about 150 yards away. Ship broke in two between third and fourth funnel. Stern section fell back horizontal, then tipped and plunged.

And so it went, account after account, all describing the same sequence: a break or fracture of the hull . . . the forward part disappearing from view . . . the afterpart righting itself briefly, then tilting up on end and plunging down too. A similar story was told by two young First Class passengers who did not testify at the hearings but left detailed accounts of their experiences. Jack Thayer and Dick Williams jumped near the end and witnessed the sinking from the water. Their recollections are subject to the same caveats as Lightoller's, but deserve no less attention. Both felt the *Titanic* was buckling or breaking up just before she sank. Thayer's view is erroneously depicted by a drawing that has been attributed to him, but was really sketched by L. D. Skidmore, a passenger on the *Carpathia*.

Colonel Gracie suggested that all these eye-witnesses

were misled by the toppling of the first funnel, which fell over as the final plunge began. Crashing into the sea in a shower of sparks, the Colonel contended, it made the whole ship appear to be breaking up. But this explanation is highly unlikely. The accounts came from thirteen different vantage points—every possible angle—and included details which couldn't reasonably be attributed to a collapsing smokestack.

But the falling funnel does lead to one more argument supporting the theory that the *Titanic* was breaking up at the end. There is a great deal of evidence about the first funnel—it barely missed Lightoller, Bride, and the other survivors on Collapsible B. Far less known is the evidence that the fourth funnel, too, collapsed in these final minutes. Trimmer Thomas Dillon, standing on the poop, watched it "cant up and fall aft toward the well deck."

No experts were needed to evaluate what happened next. The sorriest chapter of the night was the failure of ship's half-empty lifeboats to heed the cries that rose from the sea. The only excuse is that sheer terror overwhelmed every other instinct.

Take the case of No. 8, one of the portside boats launched by Second Officer Lightoller. After he loaded it with all the women and children he could see, there were still about 30 empty places. The wives began begging Captain Smith, who was standing nearby, to let in some of the husbands to row. But the old Captain backed Lightoller to the hilt—the rule was "Women and children only." So the boat was lowered and rowed away half-full, with the women still pleading for their men.

Yet after the sinking, many of these very same wives

joined the great cry of protest that went up when Seaman Thomas Jones, in charge, proposed to row back and help the people struggling in the water. Hardly anyone wanted to go, and finally the three men at the oars flatly refused to row. Miss Gladys Cherry, an English passenger handling the tiller, was one of the few willing to try, and she later wrote Jones a letter describing her anguish:

> The dreadful regret I shall always have, and I know you share with me, is that we ought to have gone back to see whom we could pick up. But if you remember, there was only an American lady, my cousin, self, and you who wanted to return. I could not hear the discussion very clearly, as I was at the tiller, but every one forward and the three men refused. But I shall always remember your words, "Ladies, if any of us are saved, remember I wanted to go back. I would rather drown with them than leave them."

Miss Cherry tended to see the dispute in terms of nationality, proudly pointing out that of the four who wanted to go back, three were English, but that was a little unfair. The most glaring case of the night involved Boat 1—only 12 people in space that could hold 40—and by far the dominant person in that boat was Sir Cosmo Duff Gordon, an Englishman to the core. Yet No. 1 did nothing, prompting Lord Mersey to give Sir Cosmo a mild rebuke in the final report of the British Inquiry.

As the cries in the water died away, Boat 8 resumed rowing toward a light that hovered all night on the northern horizon. It never seemed to get nearer, nor did it ever seem to go away—a tantalizing lure, always just out of reach. Finally, about 3:30 A.M., somebody spotted the flash of a rocket far to the southeast, followed by the lights of a new ship rapidly approaching. With relief, No. 8 stopped chasing the will-o'-the-wisp to the north, swung around, and headed for this fresh and more promising beacon of hope.

CHAPTER XIII

"The Electric Spark"

The rockets and lights to the southeast signaled the entrance of a brand-new character on the stage—a man often overlooked in recent accounts of the disaster, yet one who in many ways symbolized the robust virtues of the period.

Captain Arthur H. Rostron, commanding the Cunard Liner *Carpathia*, brought to the job a driving spirit that was woefully lacking in the *Titanic* crewmen who lay on their oars, listening to the cries of the swimmers. Born in 1869, Rostron went to sea at 13, spent ten years in sail, joined Cunard, and then rose steadily up the company ladder. Now, at 42, he was an experienced, respected shipmaster, known for his quick decisions and for his ability to transmit his own boundless energy into those serving under him. Not surprisingly, his Cunard shipmates nicknamed him "The Electric Spark."

His other most notable quality was piety. Rostron did not smoke or drink, never used profanity, and frequently turned to prayer. When he did so, he would lift his uniform cap slightly, and his lips would move in silent supplication.

In January 1912 he became Captain of the 13,564-ton *Carpathia*—less than a third the size of the huge *Titanic,* but his most important command to date. On the night of April 14–15, she was three days out of New York on a Mediterranean cruise, and so far there had been little occasion for either prayers or quick decisions.

All that ended at 12:35 A.M., when Harold Cottam, the *Carpathia's* wireless operator, burst into the Captain's quarters to report that the *Titanic* had struck a berg and urgently needed help. Rostron's reaction was completely in character. He immediately ordered the *Carpathia* turned around, then asked Cottam if he was sure. Nine out of ten captains would have done it the other way around.

The *Titanic* was 58 miles to the northwest; the *Carpathia's* maximum speed was 14 knots—meaning she could get there in four hours. That time must not be wasted. Calling his department heads to the bridge, Rostron rattled off a stream of orders. Later he wrote them up for the U.S. Senate investigation. Although prepared when he was no longer under pressure, the resulting document gives such a remarkable picture of his quick mind at work—thinking of everything—that it seems worth quoting in full:

> English doctor, with assistants, to remain in first-class dining room.
> Italian doctor, with assistants, to remain in second-class dining room.
> Hungarian doctor, with assistants, to remain in third-class dining room.

Each doctor to have supplies of restoratives, stimulants, and everything to hand for immediate needs of probable wounded or sick.

Purser, with assistant purser and chief steward, to receive the passengers, etc., at different gangways, controlling our own stewards in assisting *Titanic* passengers to the dining rooms, etc.; also to get Christian and surnames of all survivors as soon as possible to send by wireless.

Inspector, steerage stewards, and master at arms to control our own steerage passengers and keep them out of the third-class dining hall, and also to keep them out of the way and off the deck to prevent confusion.

Chief steward: That all hands would be called and to have coffee, etc., ready to serve out to all our crew.

Have coffee, tea, soup, etc., in each saloon, blankets in saloons, at the gangways, and some for the boats.

To see all rescued cared for and immediate wants attended to.

My cabin and all officers' cabins to be given up. Smoke rooms, library, etc., dining rooms, would be utilized to accommodate the survivors.

All spare berths in steerage to be utilized for *Titanic*'s passengers, and get all our own steerage passengers grouped together.

Stewards to be placed in each alleyway to reassure our own passengers, should they inquire about noise in getting our boats out, etc., or the working of engines.

To all I strictly enjoined the necessity for order, discipline, and quietness and to avoid all confusion.

Chief and first officers: All the hands to be called; get coffee, etc. Prepare and swing out all boats.

All gangway doors to be opened.

Electric sprays in each gangway and over side.

A block with line rove hooked in each gangway.

A chair sling at each gangway, for getting up sick or wounded.

Boatswains' chairs. Pilot ladders and canvas ash bags to be at each gangway, the canvas ash bags for children.

Cargo falls with both ends clear; bowlines in the ends, and bights secured along ship's sides, for boat ropes or to help the people up.

Heaving lines distributed along the ship's side, and gaskets handy near gangways for lashing people in chairs, etc.

Forward derricks; topped and rigged, and steam on winches; also told off officers for different stations and for certain eventualities.

Ordered company's rockets to be fired at 2:45 A.M. and every quarter of an hour after to reassure *Titanic*.

As each official saw everything in readiness, he reported to me personally on the bridge that all my orders were carried out, enumerating the same, and that everything was in readiness.

Yet all these measures didn't cover the biggest problem Rostron had to face—ice. If the *Titanic* had hit a berg, so could the *Carpathia*. He was going full steam into the very same region. What could be done to minimize the risk to his own ship, to his own passengers and crew?

Reducing speed was out of the question; time was everything. So Rostron took the only course left: he greatly strengthened his lookout. He added a man to the crow's nest; he put two men on the bow; he stationed a man on each wing of the bridge—all chosen for their keen eyesight. Since he was always on the bridge himself, there were now seven pairs of eyes searching the sea ahead.

Finally, one last measure, even more important than the lookout. As Second Officer James Bisset peered into the night from the starboard wing of the bridge, he suddenly became aware of Rostron standing nearby. In his familiar way, the Captain had raised his cap a couple of inches above his head, and his lips were moving in silent prayer.

At 2:45 A.M. Bisset spotted the first berg—about a mile ahead—revealed by, of all things, the reflected light of a star. The *Carpathia* steered around it and raced on. In the next hour and a quarter she dodged five more bergs, all sighted first by the bridge, suggesting that the crow's nest was not the best place to be when searching for ice at night.

At 4 A.M. the *Carpathia* reached the *Titanic*'s position, and Rostron cut his engines. He had made his run in 3½ hours—30 minutes better than his original estimate. For some time he had been watching an occasional green light ahead that would flare up briefly, then fade into the dark again. At first he thought it might be the *Titanic* herself, but now as the *Carpathia* glided to a stop, he saw it again, close and low in the water. It was a lifeboat.

Rostron eased the *Carpathia* toward the boat, trying to pick it up on his port side, which was to leeward; but as

he turned he suddenly saw one more iceberg directly
ahead and only 400 yards off. It forced him to turn back
and take the boat instead on his starboard side. It was
the only thing he did all night that didn't work out exactly as he planned.

The boat was No. 2, Fourth Officer Boxhall in charge.
He had brought along the green flares with the hope
that they might be useful in keeping the *Titanic*'s boats
together and perhaps serve as a marker for some approaching rescue ship. Now that rescue ship was here,
and Boxhall was quickly escorted to the bridge, where
he confirmed what Rostron, with sinking heart, already
sensed—the *Titanic* had sunk.

By this time day was breaking, revealing the *Titanic*'s
whole fleet of lifeboats scattered over a four-mile area.
More than that, dawn also revealed a fantastic setting.
Two or three miles to the west lay an enormous ice field,
running generally northeast to southwest, as far as the
eye could see. Here and there it was studded with individual bergs, some 200 feet high. To the east and south
lay other bergs, scattered haphazardly along the course
the *Carpathia* had just completed.

Even with a sharp lookout few of these bergs had
been sighted, and it seemed incredible that the ship had
missed them all. Years later, Rostron told his friend
Captain Barr of the Cunarder *Caronia*, "When day
broke, and I saw the ice I had steamed through during
the night, I shuddered, and could only think that some
other Hand than mine was on that helm during the
night."

Then he was "The Electric Spark" again. For the next
four hours Rostron methodically picked up the *Titanic*'s

boats one by one. The survivors came aboard by ladder, chair slings, canvas ash bags, and cargo falls with bowlines carefully knotted at the ends. All depended on how agile the person was.

As they came aboard, the survivors were processed in almost assembly-line fashion. First, names and class were taken by a purser stationed at each gangway . . . next, they were handed to the doctors for a quick medical check . . . then on down the line for brandy, coffee, breakfast, blankets, and a bunk. The *Carpathia*'s own First Class passengers gave up their cabins to those who seemed in the greatest need; the ship's public rooms were turned into dormitories for the rest. Not surprisingly, Mrs. Astor, Mrs. Widener, and Mrs. Thayer— Rostron's three most prominent guests—were assigned to his own quarters.

By 8:30 A.M. the last boat had been gathered in. The Leyland Liner *Californian* was alongside now, and Rostron asked her to search the area for anyone he might have missed. Then he turned the *Carpathia* for New York.

But before leaving the scene, Rostron added one last characteristic touch. As the *Carpathia* passed over the grave of the *Titanic*, rescuers and rescued alike assembled in the First Class dining saloon for a brief service in memory of those who were lost and in thanksgiving for those who were saved.

By the time the *Carpathia* reached New York on the evening of April 18, the city was frantic with anxiety. It was abundantly clear that a dreadful disaster had happened—some 1,500 lives lost—but no one knew much beyond that. The rescue ship's primitive wireless had a

range of only 250 miles, and her lone operator, Harold
Cottam, was exhausted. With Harold Bride's help, he
managed to tap out a list of those saved, but not much
else. Incoming queries were simply ignored, even a message from President Taft inquiring about his military
aide, Archie Butt.

Now, as she paused off Ambrose to pick up a pilot, the
Carpathia was met by a swarm of tugs, ferries, yachts,
and assorted harbor craft. Some carried huge placards
bearing the names of missing friends or relatives; others
were filled with reporters shouting questions through
megaphones. Rostron allowed none aboard, feeling that
the survivors were still in no shape to be interviewed.
When one newsman did manage to jump on the ship off
Quarantine, he was promptly collared and put under
"house arrest" on the bridge.

The uproar continued as the Carpathia crept up the
harbor, and when she again paused, this time to deliver
to the White Star Line 13 of the Titanic's lifeboats, photographers added to the din. Night photography was in
its infancy, and to catch the scene it was necessary to set
off great blasts of magnesium powder.

To cap the tumult, a cannonade of thunder and lightning rolled across the smoky sky, adding an almost
apocalyptic touch to the night. Slowly the Carpathia was
warped into Pier 54; the survivors began tottering
ashore; and at last the world could learn the full story.

Even before he set foot on land, Captain Rostron
found himself an instant hero. His calm self-assurance,
his acceptance of risks, his faith in God, his enormous
accomplishment were all immediately apparent. The
paraphernalia of heroism would follow soon enough—

scrolls, testimonial dinners, loving cups, a medal from Congress especially struck in his honor. "The Electric Spark" was well on his way to a splendid career that would ultimately see him knighted and named Commodore of the whole Cunard fleet.

CHAPTER XIV

"A Certain Amount of Slackness"

Nine hours after the *Carpathia*'s turbulent arrival in New York, the Leyland Liner *Californian* crept without fanfare into Boston Harbor early on the morning of April 19. No tugs swarmed around her; no press boats jockeyed for position; no photographers set off blasts of magnesium powder.

The *Californian* was a 6,223-ton cargo liner sailing without passengers on the unglamorous Liverpool-Boston run. She had been the second rescue ship to reach the *Titanic*'s position, but it was now known that she carried no survivors. There was only a baseless rumor that she had picked up some bodies . . . which accounted for the small knot of ship's reporters waiting silently on her Clyde Street pier.

At 7 A.M. the gangplank was lowered, and the local agent of the Leyland Line strode aboard. He went at once to the Captain's quarters, where he was closeted for some minutes with the ship's master, Captain Stanley Lord. Then the reporters were allowed on board too, and Captain Lord held what today would be called a press conference. He explained that on the evening of April 14–15 the *Californian* had been stopped by a great ice field; that the wireless was shut down for the night; and that she received her first news of the *Titanic* at 5:30 A.M. on the 15th from the Allan Liner *Virginian*.

Although 30 miles away, Captain Lord told the Boston *Evening Globe*, the *Californian* started for the scene as quickly as possible. "At best, however, it was slow going. At times, nervous and anxious as we were, we hardly seemed to be moving. We had to dodge the big bergs, skirt the massed field ice, and plow through the line of least resistance. For three full hours we turned, twisted, doubled on our course—in short, manoeuvred one way or another—through the winding channels of the ice."

Most of the reporters were suitably impressed. The *Globe* observed, "It took some mighty good seamanship to pilot the freighter through the narrow winding channels of ice, and although her officers used every effort to keep her going as fast as possible, there were times when circumstances made it necessary for her to proceed at snail's pace."

Only the *Evening Transcript* sensed that all was not quite right. Its man noted that when the reporters asked questions regarding latitude and longitude, Captain Lord said that they were requesting "state secrets," and that information would have to come from the company's office. "Ordinarily," the *Transcript*'s reporter dryly observed, "figures giving exact position in latitude and longitude have always been obtainable from the ship's officers."

The reporter was also unable to get anything out of the *Californian's* wireless operator, Cyril Evans, and caustically remarked, "So far as was apparent, his vocal organs were not impaired." Finally, the paper wondered about that private meeting between Captain Lord and the company agent just before the newsmen were allowed on board. "Possibly nothing transpired beyond regular routine business. . . ."

"Possibly." But far more likely, the reporter's skepticism was sound, for the *Californian's* voyage had been anything but routine. The complications began on the evening of April 14 during Third Officer Charles V. Groves's 8:00 to 12:00 watch. At 10:21 Groves suddenly sighted several white patches in the water ahead, which he took to be a school of porpoises crossing the bows.

Captain Lord knew better. The *Californian* had been warned of ice ahead, and here it was. Lord yanked the engine room telegraph to FULL SPEED ASTERN. As the ship lost her way, the white patches turned into flat pieces of field ice, which soon surrounded the vessel completely. There was no telling how far it stretched or how thick it was, but Captain Lord had never been in field ice before, and he was taking no chances. He decided to stick here for the night.

Leaving instructions to be called if anything was sighted, he stopped the ship, put the engines on standby, and went below. "Absolute peace and quietness now prevailed," Groves later recalled, "save for brief snatches of 'Annie Laurie' from an Irish voice, which floated up through a stokehold ventilator."

Around 11:00 Groves noticed the lights of a distant steamer coming up from the southeast. As it drew closer, he decided it was a large passenger ship. The stranger

stopped about 11:40, and seemed to put out many of its
lights. Groves remembered serving on a liner where the
lights were turned down at midnight to encourage the
passengers to go to bed, and decided that was the case
here. It did not occur to him at the time that perhaps the
lights only seemed to go out, that actually the ship had
made a hard turn to port.

Captain Lord was watching the ship too, from the
deck below, but she didn't look like a passenger liner to
him: "She was something like ourselves—a medium-
sized steamer." He asked Wireless Opeator Cyril Evans
what ships were nearby, and Evans said, "Only the *Titanic*." Lord then told him to warn her that the *Californian* was stopped and surrounded by ice. Evans tried,
but received his famous brush-off from Jack Phillips:
"Shut up, shut up. I'm busy. I'm working Cape Race."

At 11:45 Captain Lord joined Groves on the upper
bridge, and they briefly conferred about the stranger. It
was all very inconclusive. The Third Officer still believed she was a passenger ship; Lord still felt she was a
freighter. Groves thought she was a big ship maybe ten
miles away; the Captain thought she was a small ship
maybe five miles away. On Lord's instructions, Groves
had tried calling her up on the Morse lamp, but could
get no answer. Then the Captain went below again, while
Groves continued with his "morsing."

At 12:00 Groves handed over the watch to Second
Officer Herbert Stone. As Stone passed the wheelhouse
on his way to the upper bridge, he met Captain Lord,
who pointed out the strange ship and told Stone to let
him know at once if she came any closer.

On the bridge, Groves also pointed out the ship to

Stone and said he had tried calling her up on the Morse lamp without any luck. At 12:15 Groves went below, stopping by the wireless room, where he liked to tinker with the set. But Evans was now off-duty and ready to sleep, and Groves didn't know how to make the receiver work. He twiddled with the dials for a moment, then gave up and went to bed—thus missing not only a little practice but a chance to catch the *Titanic's* first call for help.

On the bridge, Stone was now joined by a 20-year-old apprentice named James Gibson, who took over the fruitless task of trying to contact the strange ship. Both men later said she looked like a tramp steamer, although Gibson also noted that there was a glare of lights on her afterdeck—a feature not at all characteristic of a tramp steamer in mid-Atlantic.

In a little while Gibson went below on routine duty; he was gone for most of the next half-hour. Stone remained on the upper bridge, handling the watch alone. At 12:40 Captain Lord called up on the speaking tube from his cabin, asking whether the other ship was any closer. No, replied Stone, all the same as before. Satisfied, Lord said he was going to the chart room and "lie down a bit" on the settee. Stone resumed his monotonous study of the night.

At 12:45 he was startled by the sudden flash of a rocket bursting over the stranger. He wasn't sure at first, but then came another, and he was certain now—white rockets, bursting in the sky, sending down a shower of white stars. After several minutes he saw another . . . and another . . . and yet another.

Five rockets altogether—enough to stir anyone to action. Stone whistled down the speaking tube, and Captain Lord was soon on the other end. Stone told him about the rockets, and Lord asked if they were private signals. "I don't know," Stone replied, "but they were all white."

The Captain then told him to try the Morse lamp again. "When you get an answer," he added, "let me know by Gibson." Lord then returned to the chart room settee and lay down once more. Later he claimed that Stone told him of only one rocket, but said that he had been sleeping soundly and had no reason to doubt Stone's version of the exchange.

Just about this time, Apprentice Gibson rejoined Stone on the upper bridge. Stone told him about the five rockets, and for a few minutes they watched the other ship together. Gibson then went back to the Morse lamp and signaled continuously for three minutes. He then focused his binoculars on her, hoping for an answer. Instead, he saw a sixth rocket. Thanks to the glasses, he had an almost perfect view: a white detonating flash . . . a faint streak upward into the sky . . . then a burst of white stars.

Stone saw the rocket too, but without the details caught by Gibson's binoculars. Then, a few minutes later both men saw a seventh, and at 1:40, an eighth and final rocket. All burst over the other ship, and even with the naked eye both men could see the white stars floating down.

Through it all—and for another 20 minutes—Stone and Gibson talked, puzzled, pondered, and sometimes differed over what they were watching. Judging by the fragments that have survived, the two men had surely one of the most remarkable conversations in the history of the North Atlantic.

"A ship is not going to fire rockets at sea for nothing," Stone observed, as the two men studied the other vessel. Gibson agreed. Stone added, Gibson later recalled, that there must be something the matter with her. The young apprentice again agreed. In fact, he thought it was a case of "some sort of distress."

"Have a look at her now, Gibson," Stone broke in as they continued to watch the stranger, still firing her rockets. "She seems to look queer now."

Gibson raised his glasses and replied, "She looks rather to have a big side out of the water." She seemed to be listing to starboard, and that glare of lights on her afterdeck looked higher than before.

Stone agreed.

Completing the picture, the stranger was now disappearing. Stone said she had begun to steam away to the southwest about the time she fired her first rocket; he noted that she was now changing her bearings. Gibson never noticed any change in the bearings—he left such calculations to Stone—but he, too, noted that she was gradually disappearing. For a long while she continued to show her red light, but never her green, as might have been expected of a ship steaming off to the southwest.

By 2 A.M. she was almost gone. Stone now told Gibson to wake up the Captain, tell him that the ship they were watching was steaming away to the southwest—that the *Californian* herself was heading west-southwest—and that the stranger had fired eight white rockets altogether.

Gibson went below, entered the chart room, and gave

the message to Captain Lord. "All right," the Captain said. "Are you sure there were no colors in them?"

"No, they were all white."

Lord then asked the time. Gibson replied that it was 2:05 "by the wheelhouse clock."

The Captain later said that he had been sleeping heavily and didn't remember any of this conversation— just a vague recollection of Gibson opening the door, saying something, and then leaving. Gibson was certain that Lord was awake the whole time.

On the bridge again, Stone and Gibson resumed studying the night. Later, there was some dispute as to exactly when the stranger disappeared. Gibson felt she was already gone by 2:05, when he reported to the Captain; Stone said she was still faintly in sight until 2:20; then her lights faded away completely.

Around 2:40 he again whistled down the speaking tube. Once more Captain Lord got up from the chart room settee, crossed to his own room, and answered the call. Stone told him that there were no more rockets, that the other ship had disappeared into the southwest and was completely out of sight. One final time, Lord asked if Stone was sure there were no colors in the rockets; one final time, the Second Officer said they were all white, "just white rockets."

At the British Inquiry the question arose as to what Stone really meant when he instructed Gibson to tell the Captain that the strange ship had "disappeared." Did he mean "gone to the bottom" or "steamed away"? Stone maintained that he meant "steamed away," but Gibson wouldn't say how *he* interpreted it. Pressed for an answer, he remained silent.

In any case, the stranger was gone. Stone and Gibson

resumed their watch, and nothing happened for the next 40 minutes—just the stars, the flat, icy sea, the empty night. Then at 3:20 A.M. Gibson suddenly saw a new rocket—more to the south and much farther away than the earlier ones. He reported it to Stone, and the two men watched as a second, and then a third rocket burst in the sky. The ship firing them was out of sight, below the horizon, but it's worth noting that at this time the *Carpathia* was racing up from the south firing rockets, trying to reassure the *Titanic* that help was coming. Strangely, Stone did not report these new rockets to Captain Lord at all.

At 4 A.M. Chief Officer George F. Stewart arrived on the upper bridge to take over the watch. Stone filled him in on the original eight rockets . . . described how the ship firing them began to steam away after the first rocket went up . . . pointed out that he had informed Captain Lord three different times.

Stewart raised his binoculars and spotted to the south a four-masted steamer with one funnel and "a lot of lights amidship." He asked Stone if that was the vessel that had been firing the rockets. No, said Stone, adding that this was a brand-new steamer he hadn't seen before.

Stone now went below, leaving the Chief Officer to sort things out. To every sailor, rockets at sea normally mean distress, and Stewart was no exception. He had an uneasy feeling that "something had happened." Yet he did nothing until 4:30 A.M., when Captain Lord had asked to be awakened. Stewart did this personally, and standing by the chart room door, he remarked that Stone had seen rockets during his watch.

"Yes, I know; he's been telling me," replied Lord.

The Captain now went on the bridge and began explaining his plans for getting through the ice and proceeding on to Boston. Stewart asked if he wasn't going
to go south first and try to learn something about the
ship that had been firing rockets. Lord raised his binoculars and looked at the four-masted steamer. "No," he
said, "she looks all right; she's not making any signals
now."

But this, of course, was not the ship that Stone had
watched. This was the newcomer that he hadn't even
seen, until pointed out by Stewart. Her condition—good
or bad—was irrelevant. Nevertheless, Stewart did not
tell the Captain that he was looking at the wrong ship.
Asked at the British Inquiry why he failed to do so, he
said he didn't know.

Little is known of Stewart's and Lord's conversation
over the next 50 minutes. At the Inquiry, Stewart said
nothing about it; Lord said only that he learned for the
first time that there was more than one rocket—something impossible to reconcile with the accounts of Stone,
Gibson, and Stewart himself.

In any event, at 5:20 life on the *Californian* suddenly
took on a much faster pace. Stewart burst into the radio
room and shook awake the operator, Cyril Evans:
"Wireless, there's a ship been firing rockets in the night.
Will you see if you can find out what is wrong—what is
the matter?"

Evans needed no further prodding. Normally he arose
at 7:00, but now he bolted out of bed and flicked on the
set. One after another, the *Mount Temple*, the *Frankfurt*,
and the *Virginian* told him about the *Titanic*, and at 5:45
he had an official message from the *Virginian*, giving

him the *Titanic's* position, 41°46' N, 50°14'W. The *Californian's* position was 42°5'N, 50°7'W—about 19 miles away.

By 6:00–6:15 Captain Lord had the *Californian* under weigh, but at the start it was very slow going. For the first three or four miles she crept westward and southward through heavy field ice, often studded with bergs. By 7:00 she was in open water again and steaming south at 13 knots, her full speed. Around 7:30 Captain Lord calculated he was at the *Titanic's* position, but found only the *Mount Temple*. She, too, had found nothing, but both ships could see the *Carpathia* stopped five or six miles to the east.

Wireless traffic indicated that the *Carpathia* was picking up the *Titanic's* boats; so Captain Lord headed for her. There was too much ice to steer a direct course; therefore, the *Californian* continued south until she found a channel in the ice, then wriggled through it, and finally approached the *Carpathia* from the southwest, or almost the opposite direction from the way she had started out. When he first noticed her, Captain Rostron estimated that the *Californian* was five or six miles to the west-southwest.

By now everyone on the *Californian* had been alerted. Extra lookouts were posted at the bow and in a coal basket hoisted above the crow's nest. Seamen were swinging her boats out for rescue work. Awakened by Chief Officer Stewart, Third Officer Groves paused long enough to ask Second Officer Stone if it was really true about the *Titanic*. "Yes, old chap," Stone replied, "I saw rockets in my watch."

By 8:30 the *Californian* was alongside the *Carpathia*,

just in time to watch Rostron pick up Boat 12, the last of the *Titanic*'s lifeboats. The two ships exchanged signals by wigwag, with the *Californian* agreeing to continue the search, while the *Carpathia* headed back for New York.

It was a disheartening search—no more survivors, not even any victims in sight, just seven abandoned lifeboats, some planks, deck chairs, a few pilasters, and a number of green cushions floating around.

The *Californian* finally gave up the search and once more headed for Boston. Like everything else on this most disputatious of voyages, there was disagreement over when she resumed her journey. Captain Lord thought it was at 11:20 A.M., after a thorough check of the whole area; Third Officer Groves thought it was around 10:40, after the most cursory of investigations. The log backed up Captain Lord, but it was hardly a reliable document. It contained not one word about any of the rockets seen during the night.

Yet that seemed to be the party line when the *Californian* arrived in Boston on the morning of April 19. No one had seen anything—no rockets, no lights, nothing unusual on the night of the 14th–15th.

And for a while the strategy worked. The Boston press virtually ignored the *Californian* on April 21, 22, and 23. She lay quietly at her Clyde Street pier, discharging and taking on cargo without the benefit of reporters or other nosy people.

Yet behind the scenes the waterfront seethed with excitement. It turned out that besides Stone and Gibson, at least one other member of the crew had seen those rockets. In particular, Ernest Gill, assistant on one of the ship's "donkey engines," had watched them go up while

out on deck taking a midnight smoke. Then Evans,
Stone, and Gibson, though silent now, had talked a lot
during the days just before the ship reached Boston.
Secondhand versions of their experiences spread
through the dockside bars.

On April 21 the ship's carpenter, W. F. McGregor,
visited his cousin John H. G. Frazer in Clinton, Massa-
chusetts, and could contain himself no longer. A reporter from the Clinton *Daily Item* was present, and on
the 23rd the paper broke the story. It told how the
watch on the *Californian* saw the rockets sent up by the
Titanic. . . .

The officer on watch, it is said, reported this to the
captain of the boat, but he failed to pay any attention to the signals, excepting to tell the watch to
keep his eye on the boat. At this time the two boats
were about ten miles apart. It being in the night, the
wireless operator on the *Californian* was asleep at
the time.

It is said that those on board the *Californian* could
see the lights of the *Titanic* very plainly, and it is also
reported that those on the *Titanic* saw the *Californian*. Finally the first mate on the *Californian*, who
with several of the officers had been watching the
Titanic, decided that he would take a hand in the
situation and so roused the wireless operator, and
an attempt was made to communicate with the *Titanic*. It was then too late. . . .

Curiously, two days passed before the Boston papers
picked up the *Daily Item*'s scoop, but rumors continued
to spread. On the 24th the *Post* finally caught a whiff,

and published an interview with Captain Lord, who denied that the *Californian* had seen anything unusual. She was only 20 miles away, he said, but sighted "no rockets or other signals of distress."

On the 25th the *Morning Globe* carried Carpenter McGregor's account, as it had appeared in the *Daily Item*. This brought another rash of denials from the embattled *Californian*. "The story is perfectly absurd," declared J. H. Thomas, agent of the Leyland Line in Boston. Captain Lord and his officers stuck to their guns: "None of the crew yesterday would say they had seen any signals of distress or any lights on the night of Sunday, April 14. One of them said he did not believe anyone else did."

Later that morning the Boston *American* exploded a bombshell that went far beyond mere gossip. The paper carried a sworn affidavit, signed by the assistant donkeyman, Ernest Gill, relating what he had seen on the night of April 14–15. Boiled down, Gill's affidavit declared that shortly before midnight he had noticed the lights of a very large steamer about ten miles away going along at full steam. He then went below but couldn't get to sleep. Coming back on deck for a smoke, he saw no sign of the big steamer, but on the horizon in the same general direction he watched two white rockets burst in the sky. He did not report this to the bridge because "they could not have helped but see them."

Once again the press descended on Captain Lord. What did he have to say now?

"A lie." . . . "Bosh." . . . "Poppycock," the Captain told various interviewers, noting that Gill had been paid $500 for his account. Chief Officer Stewart, Second Officer

Stone, and an unnamed quartermaster all backed the skipper up. Questioned by the *Herald*'s man, "Stone emphatically denied that he had notified Captain Lord of any rockets, as he had seen none, nor had any been reported to him."

But by now nobody was really listening—the show had moved to Washington. On the 25th, Captain Lord, Wireless Operator Evans, and Gill himself were all summoned to testify at the Senate hearings. Queried before he caught the train, Lord assured the Boston *Journal*, "If I go to Washington, it will not be because of this story in the paper, but to tell the Committee why my ship was drifting without power, while the *Titanic* was rushing under full speed. It will take about ten minutes to do this."

It would take far longer than ten minutes—and more than a gratuitous slap at Captain Smith—to get the *Californian* off the hook. On the afternoon of April 26, the Senate Committee heard in turn Gill, Lord, and Evans . . . and ultimately rejected the Captain's version of events. Putting all the evidence together, the Committee found that the *Californian* was less than 19 miles away, saw the *Titanic*'s rockets, and "failed to respond to them in accordance with the dictates of humanity, international usage, and the requirements of law."

Meanwhile the *Californian*'s conscience-stricken carpenter, McGregor, had not been idle. It was his interview in the *Daily Item*—not Gill's affidavit, as generally supposed—that raised the first serious charges against Captain Lord and his officers. Now he added fuel to the fire with a letter to a friend in England making pretty much the same points. The letter soon came to the attention of a London civil engineer named Gerard Jensen, who decided it was his "public duty" to pass on the contents at once to the Board of Trade. In this way McGregor's charges also became the basis for the British Inquiry's interest in the *Californian*.

Ultimately the Court heard not only the now-familiar stories of Captain Lord, Donkeyman Gill, and Wireless Operator Evans, but the accounts of the other characters in the drama as well: Third Officer Groves, who first saw the strange ship; Stone and Gibson, who watched the rockets go up; and Chief Officer Stewart, who was the prime mover in finally waking up Evans.

"There are inconsistencies and contradictions in the story as told by the different witnesses," concluded Lord Mersey, "but the truth of the matter is plain. . . . When she first saw the rockets, the *Californian* could have pushed through the ice to the open water without any serious risk and so have come to the assistance of the *Titanic*. Had she done so, she might have saved many if not all of the lives that were lost."

To the end of his days Captain Lord insisted that the *Californian* wasn't "there." From time to time he asked that the case be reopened, but the Board of Trade failed to find new grounds for any appeal, and there the matter stood. Gradually Lord came to be regarded by many as a sort of gallant loner fighting a huge bureaucracy— "Under the Wheels of the Juggernaut" was the title of one series of articles defending him.

Actually, Captain Lord's battle was far from lonely. He enjoyed the support of the Mercantile Marine Services Association, which looked after the interests of British ship officers; he had well-placed sympathizers in

Parliament; he could count on highly professional access to the press; he was backed by a small but articulate band of marine writers.

They come across as energetic, resourceful—and highly selective in presenting their evidence. They play up the testimony that the ship seen from the *Californian* looked like a freighter, but brush off Third Officer Groves, who always thought she was a passenger liner. Since the *Californian* was stopped for the night, they parade the witnesses who said the light seen from the *Titanic* was moving, but ignore the witnesses who always thought the light was stationary. As for the devastating conversation between Stone and Gibson while the rockets were going up, it is seldom mentioned.

Arguing that the *Titanic* gave the wrong position— that she was really much farther away—the *Californian*'s defenders offer a map, full of authoritative-looking squiggles, showing that the position given by the *Titanic* lay on the far side of an impenetrable ice field. They rarely mention another map with a much better pedigree. Plotted at the time by the U.S. Navy's Hydrographic Office, it is based on the ice reports of nine different ships, including the *Californian* herself. It depicts the ice field as lying more from the northeast to the southwest, hence putting the *Titanic*'s reported position on the near side of the field, where of course she belongs. The exact lay of the ice field is, in fact, a subject for endless speculation.

In support of the "wrong-position" theory, the *Californian*'s defenders produce endless mathematical calculations, but her own reported position is always accepted as gospel. The finders of the *Titanic* have not seen fit to reveal her exact location, but they stress that she was definitely on course. As for the *Californian*, we will never know for certain her position that night.

Estimates of distances at sea, the timing of incidents, the position and bearings of ships to one another are by their very nature imprecise—and never more so than the night the *Titanic* went down. There wasn't even a clock on the upper bridge of the *Californian*, and the startling clarity of the atmosphere made it, as Captain Lord himself later said, "a very deceiving night." Arguments about such variables can go on endlessly, reducing the search for the truth to a sort of *Titanic* version of "Trivial Pursuit."

The one element that lifts the night of April 14–15 out of the realm of the imponderable is the hard, incontrovertible fact of the rockets—what they were like, what they meant, and what people did about them. And it is here, I think, where the arguments of the *Californian*'s defenders really break down. They can say what they like, but they can't get away from those rockets.

Distress signals at night, as defined by regulations at the time, were "rockets or shells, throwing stars of any color or description, fired one at a time, at short intervals." The *Californian* saw eight such rockets at approximately the same time the *Titanic* was firing a similar number. Over the years the *Californian*'s defenders have often sought to defuse these rockets by calling them "flares." But nobody called them flares that night. They were called "rockets"—projectiles that shot up into the sky and burst, sending down a shower of white stars. Once, when Gibson happened to raise his binoculars at the right moment, he even saw the thin trail of the rocket as it soared upward.

Every officer on the *Californian,* including Captain Lord, agreed that these rockets—as seen or as described—resembled distress signals. Later it was generously suggested that the watch thought they might be company signals of some sort, but nobody thought so that night.

The two men on the bridge both suspected something was wrong. Second Officer Stone conceded he said, "A ship is not going to fire rockets at sea for nothing." Apprentice Gibson said both he and Stone felt the ship was in "trouble of some sort"; and again, "There must be something the matter with her." Gibson himself decided it was a case of "some kind of distress."

Chief Officer Stewart thought the rockets "might be distress signals" when he relieved Stone at 4 A.M. and Stone told him what he had seen. At the British Inquiry, Stewart admitted he thought "something had happened."

The *Californian* saw and ignored still more rockets fired from yet another ship that night. These rockets were seen at the very time the *Carpathia* was firing rockets as she neared the scene, and also came from her direction.

Both Stone and Gibson immediately connected the rockets with the *Titanic* while the *Californian* was en route to the scene the following morning—before there was any time for second-guessing or wishful thinking.

Captain Lord was informed. Later he said he was told of only one rocket, but he is contradicted by all three of the other men on the bridge that night.

Feeling as he did, the Captain claimed there was no need to worry. But he and Stewart were worried enough to wake up the wireless operator at 5:20 A.M. and ask him then to check. The tragedy is that this wasn't done sooner.

Some apologists argue that it would have made no difference anyhow: the *Californian* was, they say, too far away to help. They point out that neither Stone nor Gibson heard the rockets, which (we are assured) went off with a tremendous bang, easily audible for upward of ten miles. Actually, nobody knows how far the *Titanic's* rockets could be heard. A professional ballistics expert I have consulted says maybe two or three miles. In any case, the signals were *seen* and ignored.

In the face of all this, the *Californian's* defenders offer two distinct theories. The first is that there were two separate pairs of ships out there: the *Titanic* and an unknown stranger, and the *Californian* and an unknown stranger. Neither pair was in sight of the other. In each pair, one of the ships came up from the east, stopped some time between 11:30 and midnight, and later began firing rockets. In each pair, about eight rockets were fired. In each pair, the rocket-firing ship gradually disappeared, finally vanishing about 2½ hours after she first stopped. In the case of each pair, another hour passed, and then a third ship appeared firing rockets on the southern horizon. Even on this incredible night, such a string of coincidences seems too far-fetched to accept.

The second theory concedes that the rockets probably came from the *Titanic,* but contends that there was a third, unknown ship lying between the sinking liner and the *Californian.* This was the ship Stone and Gibson were watching, the theory runs, and they mistakenly believed the rockets were coming from her. Since she looked all right, they had no need to worry.

But the ship they were watching did *not* look all right, and both Stone and Gibson were very worried indeed. Whatever was said later, that night both men suspected that she was in trouble. "We were talking about it all the time," Gibson testified.

Moreover, the "ship in between" theory collides head on with Stone's explanation of why the stranger's lights "disappeared." Stone said they disappeared not because the ship he was watching sank, but because she steamed away. If that was the case, the British Court asked, why didn't the mysterious ship steam out from in front of the rockets, revealing where they were really coming from? Stone had no answer to that.

Nor has the "ship in between" ever been found. A perennial candidate is the Norwegian sealer *Samson*, based on the typescript of a journal supposedly kept by one of her crew. According to the typescript (the original has vanished) the *Samson* lay near the *Titanic*, saw the rockets, but was engaged in illegal sealing operations and was afraid to show herself.

Unfortunately, the same document puts the *Samson* south of Cape Hatteras the previous afternoon. Not even the *Mauretania*'s mighty turbines could have propelled her to the icy waters off Newfoundland in time for the big show.

Further doubt is cast on the *Samson* by some remarkable research undertaken by Leslie Reade, a little-known British *Titanic* scholar who enjoys almost guru status among students of the disaster. Mr. Reade has devel-

oped information from official sources in Iceland plac-
ing the *Samson* in the fishing port of Isafjördhur on
April 6 and again on April 20. This meant that the
Samson had just 14 days to make the 3,000-mile journey
down to the *Titanic* and back—absolutely impossible for
a six-knot ship.

In any event, what difference does it make even if
there was a third ship lying between the *Californian* and
the *Titanic*? Rockets are rockets. These clearly resembled distress signals, and both Stone and Gibson suspected some ship was in trouble.

As an ameliorating factor, it has been suggested that
they mistook the rockets for company signals—or signals between fishermen operating off the Banks of
Newfoundland. Ships did occasionally use night signals
to identify themselves in those days, but they were usually some combination of colored flares and Roman can-
dles. They did not remotely resemble the white rockets
seen by Stone and Gibson . . . or the white rockets being
fired at about that time by the *Titanic*. It didn't occur to
either man that the ship they were watching was merely
trying to identify herself. Again, they suspected that she
was trying to get help.

Finally, it has been suggested that the two men on the
bridge thought the rockets were just a celebration of
some sort. This theory grew out of a caustic remark
made at the British Inquiry by Butler Aspinwall, counsel
for the Board of Trade, while he was examining Stone
on the meaning of the rockets. Stone proved so evasive
that finally, in exasperation, Aspinwall remarked, "You
knew they were not being sent up for fun?" Somehow
this got twisted around in the retelling and has come

down to us as an explanation by Stone, rather than a bit
of sarcasm by Aspinwall.

It's a waste of time to linger any longer over the question of what Stone and Gibson thought the rockets
meant. The real question is why, when they were reported to Captain Lord, he did nothing about them.

Certainly the Captain was not drunk—he was a tee-
totaler.

Nor does it seem likely that he was too deeply asleep
to grasp the reports sent down to him. He was not tucked
away in bed; he was resting fully clothed on the chart
room settee. His rest was interrupted three different
times between 12:40 and 2:40. Twice he had to get up
and go to his own quarters to talk with Stone on the
speaking tube; the other time he was visited by Gibson
in person. All three times he seemed awake and perfectly rational. It had not been an especially difficult
day; there was no reason to be exhausted.

In the end it's hard not to be impressed by the reasoning of Sir Rufus Isaacs, the Attorney General at the
British Inquiry:

> . . . I am unable to find any possible explanation of
> what happened, except it may be the Captain of the
> vessel was in ice for the first time, and would not
> take the risk of going to the rescue of another vessel
> which might have got into trouble, as he thought,
> from proceeding through the ice when he himself
> had stopped.

It must always be remembered that the *Titanic* hadn't
happened yet. When he made up his mind to stay put,

Captain Lord had no inkling that the world's most famous sea disaster was about to occur. He only knew
there was a lot of ice out there, and the safe thing to do
was to stop for the night. This was the right decision—
provided nothing happened. But something did happen, and Captain Lord's failure was his inability or
unwillingess to adjust to an entirely new situation. True,
he had his own ship and crew to think about, but that
was no excuse for doing nothing. He didn't even wake
up his wireless operator, only a few feet away, while the
rockets were going up. What was good seamanship before the rockets became a woeful lack of enterprise afterward.

Even when summoned to Washington, Captain Lord
seemed to feel that the real issue was his prudence, rather
than his failure to answer the rockets. Hence his curious
remark that his purpose was "to tell the Committee why
my ship was drifting without power, while the *Titanic*
was rushing under full speed."

Given that mind-set, it required a forceful man to be
on watch that night—an officer not afraid to take on a
reluctant captain. There's some question as to whether
Herbert Stone was the ideal person to be in this position. While there was always a gulf between the master
and his officers in those days, it seems to have been
especially deep between Captain Lord and Second
Officer Stone. Lord was an austere autocrat; Stone was
an easygoing type. Later he reportedly told friends that
he and Gibson did indeed think that the rockets were
distress signals, but they "couldn't get the old man out
of the chart room."

How hard did they try? While Stone twice reported

the rockets to the Captain, carefully describing them each time, he never mentioned his and Gibson's misgivings about them, or ventured any opinion as to what they might mean. "I just took them as white rockets," he later told the British Inquiry, "and informed the master, and let him judge."

Chief Officer Stewart, who took over the watch at 4 A.M., was a bit of an improvement. When Captain Lord came on the bridge at 4:30 and began talking about proceeding to Boston, Stewart at least asked him if he was going to steam south first and check on the ship that had been firing rockets during the night. "No, I do not think so," Captain Lord replied, studying the ship that had recently appeared to the south. "She looks all right; she is not making any signals now."

He was, of course, looking at the wrong ship, the new arrival that Stone had specifically said was *not* the one firing the rockets. Stewart knew this but did not correct the Captain. Why, is anybody's guess. Was he, too, cowed by the remote presence of the shipmaster? Was he so concerned about the rockets that he was willing to let the new arrival be a stand-in for the real ship, so that at least some action might be taken? We'll never know. Even when pressed, he never gave the Court any explanation at all.

So, at 4:30 A.M. the situation remained essentially as it had been all night. The rockets were still ignored, and now Captain Lord was thinking only of getting on to Boston. Yet 50 minutes later, at 5:20, Stewart was shaking the wireless operator awake: "There's a ship been firing rockets. Will you see if you can find out if anything is the matter?"

What happened that turned everything around during those 50 minutes? Sometimes I wish that some magical time machine could transport me back and let me spend an hour any place I wanted on the night of April 14–15, 1912. I would not spend that hour on the *Titanic*. I'd spend it on the bridge of the *Californian*, from 4:30 to 5:30 A.M., sharing the watch with Captain Lord and Chief Officer Stewart. What was said? What ideas were exchanged? What advice was politely rendered? What suggestions were made? What thoughts were passed— or not passed—between them?

We have very little to go on. As shown by their performance in Boston, the officers of the *Californian* were anything but candid about that night. Stewart even maintained that his purpose in waking up the wireless operator was simply to check the identity of the ship to the south—an explanation emphatically rejected by the British Inquiry.

In both his interview with the Clinton *Daily Item* and his letter to London, Carpenter McGregor declared that Stewart was so exasperated at the *Californian*'s inaction that he finally woke up Evans on his own, apparently without any clearance from the Captain. This seems going too far; Captain Lord must have given at least tacit approval.

What changed his mind? My hunch is that it was not Stewart's logic or eloquence, but a complete change of circumstances. An entirely new and reassuring element had entered the picture: daylight.

By 5:20 the night was rapidly fading, and the coral tint of dawn was spreading over the sea, showing the great ice field in all its detail—the bergs, the growlers, the loose, flat cakes of the floe. It was now possible to see the channels that wound through the ice . . . and the densely packed areas where it was too thick to go. It was at last safe for a prudent man to act.

It did not have to be that way. Captain Rostron, "The Electric Spark," proved that. But the *Californian* was different—a plodding cargo liner, presided over by a cautious captain and an uninspired watch. Six months later, before attitudes had hopelessly hardened, Captain Lord wrote a letter to his "M.P." In it he admitted there was "a certain amount of 'slackness' aboard the *Californian* the night in question." He was probably thinking of Stone, but it's a word that could well serve as an epitaph for the performance of the whole ship that night—including her captain.

CHAPTER XV

Second-guessing

The bronzed men of the sea were soon gone from the stage, their place taken by a pallid cast of lawyers, bureaucrats, technical experts, and (eventually) historians. Even before the *Carpathia* reached New York, voices were rising in Washington, demanding to know how such a catastrophe could happen.

The chorus was led by Senator William Alden Smith, a man whose constituency had nothing to do with the sea; he was from Grand Rapids, Michigan, 720 miles from the Atlantic Coast. Nor was he an expert on nautical matters; he was a railroad lawyer. But Senator Smith knew a hot political issue when he saw one, and here was an event that couldn't help but give him instant national exposure.

Nominally a Republican, Smith was at heart a maverick, fitting into neither the stand-pat nor progressive wings of the party. He did have populist leanings—liked to battle the trusts—and this penchant may have influenced him now. After all, the White Star Line was an integral part of Pierpont Morgan's shipping combine. Smith also liked playing the role of a rough, unpolished country boy taking on the city slickers, and White Star's combination of British merchants and Wall Street financiers may have been too good a target to resist.

First step was to check the White House and the congressional leadership, but they had no plans of their own. Satisfied, Smith now rammed through the Senate a resolution directing the Committee on Commerce to name a subcommittee to investigate the disaster. Then a quick meeting with Senator Knute Nelson, chairman of the Commerce Committee, and by noon on April 17th the subcommittee was in existence. To no one's surprise, Smith headed it up.

Characteristically, he saw to it that the six other members of the subcommittee were chosen without regard to any nautical knowledge. All he wanted was political balance. Hence there were three Republicans and three Democrats, with each party supplying a conservative, a liberal, and a moderate.

The most daring feature was the subpoena powers granted the subcommittee. After all, many of the key witnesses would be British. No one was sure whether the subcommittee's subpoena powers extended to foreigners or not, and assuming they did, no one knew how the proud, sensitive British seafaring men would respond.

Smith took his chances, for there was no time to lose. The *Carpathia* might not answer President Taft's queries, but there was evidence that her wireless room was doing more than the forlorn business of tapping out the list of survivors. On April 17 the U.S. cruiser *Chester* intercepted an interesting message from the little Cunarder to the White Star offices in New York:

Most desirable *Titanic* crew should be returned home earliest moment possible. Suggest you hold *Cedric,* sailing her daylight Friday. . . . Propose returning in her myself. (signed) YAMSI

It did not take a team of crack cryptanalysts to figure out that "YAMSI" was Ismay spelled backward. Apparently the White Star chairman was planning to get himself and the lost liner's crew out of U.S. jurisdiction before any investigation could get started.

Smith and the subcommittee members immediately headed for New York with a small army of marshals. They arrived on the evening of April 18—just as the *Carpathia* reached Quarantine. They hurried by taxi to the Cunard pier, arriving as the rescue ship crept in amid the blaze of photo-flash explosions. As the gangplank fell in place—before even the first survivors could step ashore—the Senator and his marshals rushed aboard.

They found Ismay in the Chief Surgeon's cabin, where he had been secluded ever since his rescue Monday morning. The ship's rumor factory had him out of his mind with grief and shock, but the figure that awaited them was thoroughly composed.

No, said "YAMSI," he wouldn't dream of skipping any American inquiry. He wanted to cooperate in every way. He would certainly appear at 10 A.M. tomorrow in the Waldorf-Astoria's East Room, which had been converted into a hearing room for the subcommittee in New York.

True to his word, Ismay was already seated at the conference table when Senator Smith and his party entered the East Room the following morning. At 10:30 Smith opened the proceedings, calling on Ismay as the first witness. Would he kindly give the Committee any information he thought might be helpful, telling the story "as succinctly as possible."

Ismay quickly showed how succinct he could be. After giving the *Titanic*'s engine revolutions for each day of the voyage—and the day's run that resulted—he came to Sunday night. "I was in bed myself, asleep, when the accident happened," he explained. "The ship sank, I am told, at two-twenty. That, sir, I think is all I can tell you."

Unfazed, Smith asked what Ismay did after the impact, and perhaps for the first time the White Star Chairman realized that he was in for a grilling that would eventually add up to 58 pages of testimony.

Across the Atlantic, the British viewed the Senate investigation first with disbelief, and then with dismay. What were those cheeky Americans doing investigating a British family matter anyhow? As Joseph Conrad put it in the May 1912 issue of the *English Review*:

> . . . Why an officer of the British merchant service should answer the questions of any king, emperor, autocrat, or senator of any foreign power (as to an event in which a British ship alone was concerned, and which did not even take place in the territorial waters of that power) passes my understanding.

The fact that the *Titanic* was, after all, serving American ports and soliciting American passengers seemed to make little difference. And the fact that, after piercing the corporate veil, the White Star Line was basically an American-owned company was never even mentioned. All in all, Conrad sniffed, the Senate's intrusion was a "very provincial display of authority."

Nor did Senator Smith help his cause as the investigation unfolded. He showed almost total ignorance of ships and the sea, once asking a witness, "Did the *Titanic* go down by the head or the bow?"

His most famous gaffe occurred when he asked Fifth Officer Lowe, "Do you know what an iceberg is composed of?"

"Ice, I suppose, sir," replied Lowe, going in for the kill.

Yet Smith's question was not all that bad, considering the general lack of knowledge on both sides of the Atlantic about icebergs and what they could do. It was hard to believe that a mere piece of ice, however big, could rip apart a steel hull. Smith was wondering whether icebergs might also contain more familiar lethal material like rocks and stones. Earlier he had put the same question to Fourth Officer Boxhall, and got a straight answer: "Some people tell me that they have seen sand and gravel and rocks and things of that kind in them." That time nobody laughed. It took Lowe to see the opening and drive home the thrust.

"A born fool," concluded the London press, and contempt was added to chauvinism in the continued attack on the Senate's investigation. There was a general feeling that things would be different when the British launched their own inquiry into the tragedy. As the *Daily Telegraph* politely explained:

> The inquiry which has been in progress in America has effectively illustrated the inability of the lay mind to grasp the problem of marine navigation. It is a matter of congratulation that British custom provides a more satisfactory method of investigating the circumstances attending a wreck.

The "more satisfactory method" was a special court, convened by the Board of Trade, headed by Lord Mersey, a prominent jurist appointed by the Lord Chancellor at the Board of Trade's request. Assisting him were five "assessors," but they were in no sense associate judges; they were strictly technical experts, there to help Lord Mersey, if and when called upon. As Commissioner of Wrecks, he had the final say on everything—the matters to be investigated, the witnesses to be called, the interests that would be represented, and ultimately the findings of the Court itself.

The *Daily Telegraph* called Lord Mersey "one of the country's leading authorities on nautical affairs," but actually he was far from that. Although an experienced judge, his field was commercial law, and he had served as president of the Probate, Divorce, and Admiralty Division of the High Court for only a year. Yet he was shrewd, witty, and possessed the kind of legal mind that could readily assimilate the facts of a complicated case.

The Inquiry opened May 2 at the London Scottish Drill Hall, a great barn of a building with dreadful acoustics, but the only available place big enough to hold all who had reason to come. For 36 days the story of the *Titanic* unfolded once again, as a steady parade of witnesses were examined by counsel representing such varied interests as the White Star Line, the National Sailors and Firemen's Union, the Third Class passengers, the owners and officers of the *Californian*, and the Board of Trade itself. Over 50 lawyers were present altogether, constantly jockeying to protect or promote their clients' interests.

Through it all, Lord Mersey remained in firm command. Usually he was content to let the testimony unfold, but if he thought that it was getting nowhere, he would break in with an irritated, "This is not helping me at all." Evasive witnesses especially annoyed him. At one point in the questioning of the unfortunate Herbert Stone, Second Officer of the *Californian*, Mersey suddenly declared, "You know, you do not make a good impression upon me at present."

Above all, he did not tolerate fools gladly. During the testimony of Alexander Carlisle, designer of the *Titanic*, Carlisle described a meeting at which he and Harold Sanderson of the White Star Line were present but did not say anything. "Mr. Sanderson and I were more or less dummies," Carlisle explained.

"That has a certain verisimilitude," Lord Mersey observed.

Apart from the Commissioner's urbanity—along with an unruffled atmosphere where opposing counsel politely called one another "my good friend"—the British Inquiry differed in a less noticeable but more important way from the rough-and-tumble of the Senate's investigation. It put much more emphasis on the technical side of the disaster: the faulty design of the *Titanic*; the Board of Trade's outdated lifeboat regulations; the Board's casual acceptance of inadequate boat drill; the reckless navigation practiced by shipmasters in the competitive struggle on the North Atlantic run.

Unconsciously, through the testimony of witnesses, the Inquiry also brought out the laxity of the Board of Trade in administering its own regulations. Captain Maurice Henry Clarke, the inspector who cleared the *Titanic* for sailing, approved a "boat drill" that consisted of lowering only two lifeboats, manned by a handpicked crew, while the ship was tied up at dock. When he conceded that he had tightened his requirements since the disaster, Lord Mersey broke in:

> "Then you do not think your system before the *Titanic* disaster was very satisfactory?"
> "No, sir."
> "Did you think it satisfactory before the *Titanic* disaster?"
> "No, sir."
> "Then why did you do it?"
> "Because it was the custom."
> "Do you follow a custom because it is bad?"
> "Well, I am a civil servant, sir, and custom guides us a good bit."

Even more depressing was the testimony of Sir Alfred Chalmers, who had been Nautical Advisor to the Marine Department of the Board of Trade, 1896–1911. It was felt that he would know better than anybody else why the Board's lifeboat regulations had not been updated to reflect the enormous increase in the size of vessels since 1896. Sir Alfred, it turned out, had no interest in updating regulations; he thought there were too many already. He preferred, as far as possible, to do away with all regulations, leaving such matters as lifeboats to the "voluntary action of shipowners." He was, in short, an owner's dream: a regulator who didn't believe in regulations.

As for the *Titanic,* Chalmers declared, no lives were lost because the required number of boats had not been increased since 1896. Her problem was not too few, but too many boats. He pointed out that many of the boats had left half-filled. This was often due to complacency. If there had been fewer boats, the passengers would have been less complacent. The boats would then have left with more people in them, and ultimately more would have been saved.

While the British Inquiry explored even the murkiest minds on the technical aspects of the disaster, Lord Mersey seemed to show relatively little interest in the passengers' ordeal. Of 102 witnesses, the only passengers to testify were Sir Cosmo and Lady Duff Gordon. Along with Lady Duff Gordon's secretary, Miss Francatelli, they were among the 12 persons who left the *Titanic* in Boat 1, which was supposed to hold 40. Ugly rumors were spreading that Sir Cosmo had bribed the boat crew to row away, and now he was trying to clear himself.

On May 17 the Duff Gordons arrived at the hearings flanked by their lawyers. Attracted by the whiff of possible scandal in high places, the gallery was filled with prominent spectators, including the Earl of Clarendon, the Russian Ambassador, Prince Leopold of Battenberg, and Mrs. Asquith, wife of the Prime Minister. If they were hoping for some sensational revelation, they were in for a disappointment. Sir Cosmo convinced the Court that he had not ordered Boat 1 to row away, and that the £5 payment he later made to each member of the boat crew was simply a gift to help them buy a new kit. He had done nothing improper, and Lord Mersey's only criticism was that he might have exercised a little positive leadership at a time when the boat was drifting, largely empty, within easy reach of the hundreds struggling in the water. The Duff Gordons cleared, the Inquiry went back to its diligent probing of the causes of the wreck.

In contrast, the Senate investigation concentrated much more heavily on what might be called the human side of the disaster. Not counting Bruce Ismay, some 20 passengers from all three classes gave testimony, throwing a great deal of light on such pertinent points as the way the alarm was spread after the collision, the amount of warning given, the mustering for the boats, the different procedures followed on the port and starboard sides, the varying treatment accorded each of the three classes.

In the end, both the American and the British approaches proved useful in getting at the truth. Neither showed the "right" or the "wrong" way to conduct an investigation. Nor were they in any sense redundant. Rather, they complemented each other, together throwing a great deal of light on the disaster, and incidentally providing future students with 2,111 pages of firsthand information that would be sifted and sifted forever more.

Despite different approaches, it was not too surprising, then, that the two inquiries reached similar conclusions. Both decided that the *Titanic* was going too fast; that a good and proper lookout was not kept; that there was poor organization in loading and lowering the lifeboats; that the *Californian* was in sight, saw the rockets, and could have come; that there was no discrimination against Third Class.

Both inquiries recommended that passenger vessels should carry lifeboats for all on board; that there should be better and more frequent boat drills; that wireless operators should be on duty 24 hours a day; that steps should be taken to improve the watertight integrity of the ever-greater liners that were now sailing the seas.

In both investigations the findings on Third Class were curious. It is perhaps understandable that Lord Mersey saw no discrimination. Mr. Harbinson, officially representing Third Class interests, did not call on a single steerage survivor to testify, and he personally assured the Court that there was "not an atom or a tittle of evidence" that anyone in Third Class was held back.

Less understandable were the findings of the Senate investigation. Of the three Third Class witnesses examined, two clearly stated that members of the crew tried to keep them below. Yet, it must be conceded, they also said they did not believe they had been discriminated against. One can only conclude that steerage aspirations were low: in 1912 it was enough to be given a life belt.

There were differences, too, between the two reports. Lord Mersey's findings were definitely more cautious. Considering his cutting comments during the testimony, one might have expected some of that bite in his report, but this was not the case. "It carries reticence to the severest extreme," complained the *Daily Mail*. Even more disappointed was *Nautical Magazine*, the merchant service officer's professional journal:

> Lord Mersey's judgement in the *Titanic* inquiry leaves us very much where we were before. It is colourless, timid, and cautious. We had expected more backbone in Lord Mersey. . . .

On the question of lifeboats, for instance, Senator Smith flatly demanded that in the future there should be boats for all, passengers and crew. Lord Mersey, on the other hand, was content to say that "the accommodation should be sufficient for all persons on board, with, however, the qualification that in special cases where, in the opinion of the Board of Trade, such provision is impracticable, the requirements may be modified as the Board may think right."

The qualification created a loophole big enough for any shipowner to slip through, and left the recommendation virtually meaningless.

But the biggest difference between the two reports was on the question of Captain Smith's blame. He was so beloved—and faced his end so bravely—that it seemed almost brutal to criticize him at all. More in sorrow than in anger, Senator Smith finally blamed the Captain as gently as he could:

> Captain Smith knew the sea, and his clear eye and steady hand had often guided his ship through dangerous paths. . . . His indifference to danger was one of the direct and contributing causes to this

unnecessary tragedy. . . . Overconfidence seems to have dulled the faculties usually so alert.

Lord Mersey came to the opposite conclusion. The White Star Line had paraded 11 sea captains before the Court, all of whom testified that when there was ice ahead and the weather was good, they always went full speed until the ice was actually sighted. Captain Smith had simply done what everybody else did, and the fact that in his case the ice wasn't sighted until the ship was almost on top of it made no difference:

> I am not able to blame Captain Smith. . . . He was doing only that which other skilled men would have done in the same position. . . . He made a mistake, a very grievous mistake, but one in which, in face of the practice and of past experience negligence cannot be said to have had any part; and in the absence of negligence it is, in my opinion, impossible to fix Captain Smith with blame.

The whole question of blame was becoming more and more important, for the damage claims were now piling up. Ultimately they totaled some $16 million—which works out at about $176 million in terms of today's dollars. It was a staggering sum in 1912, an innocent era when litigants were more easily satisfied than now.

The claims for loss of life were especially revealing. The highest was for $1,000,000, filed by the widow of Henry B. Harris, the Broadway theater owner and producer. His magic touch was a unique gift that Mrs. Harris felt she couldn't possibly carry on.

At the opposite extreme, some of the wealthiest and

most socially prominent families sought nothing at all. In 1912 it seemed somehow demeaning to put a price tag on a gentleman's life, and the Astors, Wideners, Guggenheims, and Strauses filed no claims whatsoever. The Thayers did file a claim for the luggage of John B. Thayer, but nothing for the loss of his life.

As the claims poured in, the White Star Line's New York attorney, Charles C. Burlingham faced the avalanche with the sangfroid a good Wall Street lawyer can always muster in a tight corner. He had, after all, guided the imperious Bruce Ismay safely through the Senate hearings, and nothing could be much harder than that. Besides, he now had a powerful defensive weapon at his disposal—the doctrine of limited liability.

Both American and British law had long given special protection to shipowners whose vessels, through negligent handling, caused damage to others. The risks of sending ships to sea were so great that some special incentive was needed, if maritime nations were to grow and prosper. Moreover, on land the factory owner could at least theoretically oversee the acts of his employees, but the shipowner had no such control over his captain and crew. By the very nature of the business he was usually out of touch, and it seemed unfair to hold him to the same degree of responsibility when something went wrong. Therefore, as long as he did not have "privity or knowledge" of the negligence, his liability would be limited.

Limited to what? A valid question, for the two nations applied completely different formulas in computing the amount of money the White Star Line would have to divvy up to settle the claims. In England the formula was £8 ($40) per registered ton for loss of property, and £15 ($75) per registered ton for injury or loss of life. For the 46,000-ton *Titanic,* this meant a pool of about £690,000 ($3,450,000) altogether.

In America the formula was completely different. It was the total value of everything salvaged from the ship plus the money paid in by shippers and passengers who were never carried to their destinations. But the only salvage from the *Titanic* was the cluster of 13 lifeboats picked up by the *Carpathia* and brought back to New York; and the money paid by the passengers and shippers added up to less than $40,000—meaning the pool to pay off the claims would amount to just $97,772.12.

On October 8, 1912, the White Star Line formally petitioned the Federal District Court in New York for limited liability as spelled out under the American law. The claimants, whose lawyers had by now formed a loose coalition, opposed the petition, arguing that the far more generous English law should apply. Even though the forum was an American court, the argument ran, the accident occurred on the high seas where nobody had jurisdiction, and in such cases the governing law should be the law of the country where the ship was registered.

The District Court found for the White Star Line, but was reversed on appeal, and ultimately the Supreme Court itself made the final decision. It ruled that an American court could only apply American law, and therefore the White Star Line was correct in seeking limited liability under the American formula. Whether the line was justified in seeking limited liability was another matter, which would have to be decided separately.

Meanwhile there were legal battles in England too. An Irish farmer named Thomas Ryan sued in the High Court of Justice, King's Bench Division, for the loss of his son, and his lawyer argued that the doctrine of limited liability didn't even apply, because the White Star Line itself was negligent, as well as the crew of the ship. Lord Mersey had seen no negligence anywhere, but a jury of 12 independent-minded citizens found that the White Star Line was at least partly to blame for the *Titanic*'s excessive speed. Farmer Ryan was awarded £125 in damages, and the verdict was upheld on appeal.

Not surprisingly, this decision started a small rush of American claimants to the British courts, where it looked as if they might have a better chance of winning. The American courts took a benign view of this exodus—it was up to the British courts to keep order in their own house.

Most of the American claimants, however, stayed put, and on June 22, 1915, the case finally came to trial. Speaking as the White Star's chief attorney, C. C. Burlingham took the position that there was no negligence at all, but if there was, it was not the owners who were to blame; their liability should be limited to the $97,772.12 prescribed under American law.

The claimants fought back, arguing that there was indeed negligence in the handling of the ship, and the owners had a share in it through the presence of Bruce Ismay on board. He was described as virtually a supercaptain, giving orders for speed trials and the lighting of extra boilers.

Once again the picture was conjured up of the famous meeting before lunch on that fatal Sunday when Captain Smith handed Ismay the *Baltic*'s ice warning, and Ismay stuffed it into his pocket. Surely, the claimants contended, that constituted "privity or knowledge" of negligence, removing the owners from the protection of limited liability. Final arguments were heard July 27–29, and Judge Julius M. Mayer began his consideration of the case. On the surface, life settled down to a long period of silent waiting.

Beneath the surface, all was activity. It seems that C. C. Burlingham was not as confident as he sounded. His presentation was flawless, but the country was in a progressive mood, and to many people $97,772 seemed a scandalously low price for the owners of the *Titanic* to pay. Nor were the claimants free from doubt. Claims now totaled over $16 million, and some seemed extravagant or even frivolous. Certainly it didn't strengthen the credibility of the figure to have Edith Rosenbaum include $2.00 for a hot water bottle and $20 for perfume, powder, and rouge. Nor did it help to have Mary McGovern add $20 to her claim for time spent listening to highly technical arguments in court.

Who initiated the step is uncertain, but lawyers for both sides began quietly conferring in an effort to find some acceptable compromise. The claimants gradually scaled down their demands from the original $16 million to less than $3 million, while White Star began inching up the $97,772 it owed under limited liability.

On December 17, 1915, Burlingham suddenly announced that the parties were near settlement. White Star agreed to pay $664,000, to be apportioned among the claimants according to their scaled-down schedule. In return the claimants agreed to drop all suits both in

America and in England, and agreed that the White Star
Line had no "privity or knowledge" of any negligence on
the *Titanic*. This last constituted an acknowledgment that
the ship's owners were indeed protected by limited liability and presumably barred any suits in the future. The
lawyers for nearly all the claimants went along with the
deal. Only a few loose ends remained to be cleared up.

The loose ends, it turned out, took another six months.
Much of the time was spent trying to divide up equitably
the $664,000. The maximum allowed, for instance,
would be $50,000 for loss of life under certain condi-
tions—which meant that Renée Harris had to come down
quite a bit from the $1,000,000 she originally claimed.
On the other hand, the cut was far less severe for loss of
life in steerage. The average claim had been $1,500; the
average award would be $1,000.

On July 28, 1916, the settlement was formally signed
and sealed. In the end, White Star paid six times as
much as it argued that it owed under limited liability . . .
but only 22% of the scaled-down claims and less than
4% of the $16 million originally demanded. All in all,
C. C. Burlingham had not done badly by his clients.
After four years, three months, one week, and six days,
the litigation over the *Titanic* was at last a closed book.

CHAPTER XVI

Why Was Craganour
Disqualified?

The damage claims were now a closed book, but not the story of the human beings who survived the *Titanic*. Many would find their lives permanently intertwined with the disaster.

Bruce Ismay would never live it down. As Chairman and Managing Director of the White Star Line, he was ultimately responsible for the shortage of lifeboats, yet he went off in a boat, leaving hundreds stranded on the sloping decks. Captain Smith, people felt, at least had the good grace to go down with the ship. In Chicago a young newspaperman named Ben Hecht put the contrast into verse:

> The Captain stood where a captain should
> For the law of the sea is grim.
> The owner romped ere his ship was swamped
> And no law bothered him.

The Captain stood where the captain should
When a captain's boat goes down.
But the owner led when the women fled
For an owner must not drown.

The Captain sank as a man of rank
While his owner turned away.
The Captain's grave was his bridge, and brave
He earned his seaman's pay.

To hold your place in the ghastly face
Of death on the sea at night
Is a seaman's job, but to flee with the mob
Is an owner's noble right.

Even the revered naval authority Rear Admiral A. T. Mahan fired a scholarly broadside. Conceding that Ismay was in no sense responsible for the collision, Mahan argued that once the accident had occurred, Ismay was confronted with a whole new condition, for which he (and not the Captain) was responsible—namely, the shortage of lifeboats. . . .

Did no obligation as to particularity of conduct rest upon him under such a condition? I hold that under that condition, so long as there was a soul that could be saved, the obligation lay upon Mr. Ismay that that one person and not he should have been in the boat.

The storm of criticism continued. Perhaps the ultimate indignity came when the citizens of Ismay, a new town in Jackson County, Texas, decided to change the name of their community to something—anything—less ignominious. Faced with the same problem, the people of Ismay, Montana, decided to hang on: "None of us," declared the *Ismay Journal,* "need be ashamed to register from Ismay, one of the prettiest, cleanest, and most sub-stantial little towns on the entire Puget Sound Road, merely because someone of similar name has not lived up to the high standard of ethics established by some self-appointed critics." The editor even wondered whether Bruce Ismay had received a fair deal.

He was in the minority. Far more typical was the yel-low press, which began referring to "J. BRUTE Ismay."

Across the Atlantic, on April 21 a rumor spread in Liverpool that Ismay, unable to stand the strain any longer, had committed suicide in New York. Shocked at the thought, a local citizen named Charles W. Jones dashed off a bitter protest to the Foreign Office: ". . . That a British subject and an English gentleman should be put to such indignities is causing much indig-nation in Liverpool, and I now most humbly beg of you to make some representation to the United States gov-ernment on his behalf."

Actually, Ismay had his troubles with British critics too. In a feisty open letter appearing in the journal *John Bull,* editor Horace Bottomley asked him, "How is it that *you,* above all people, were in one of the lifeboats? . . . Your place was at the captain's side till every man, woman and child was safely off the ship." Most of the criticism, however, was in a lower key. "It is not given to everyone to be a hero," remarked *Nautical Magazine,* bible of the merchant service.

In the end the British Inquiry exonerated him. Lord Mersey found that Ismay was under no moral obligation to stick with the ship. The lifeboat was actually being lowered; no one else was at hand; there was room; so he jumped. "Had he not jumped in, he would have merely added one more life, namely his own, to the number of those lost." All very well, but many people found it hard to believe there weren't other passengers nearby. Ismay remained under a cloud.

For a while he fought back as best he could. Long before the *Titanic,* Ismay had planned to retire as Chairman of the White Star Line and other affiliated companies. Now that looked too much like a retreat, and he tried to stay on at least as head of White Star. The American owners would have none of it. The most they would give him was a chance to save face a little. "The decision they have reached," wrote his friend and fellow director Harold Sanderson, "is to be attributed to a considered and settled policy, and not to any personal feeling toward yourself."

On June 30, 1913, Bruce Ismay retired as Chairman of the White Star Line and began an ever-widening withdrawal from public life. He remained on a number of boards, but they were mostly honorific, and he spent much of his time at a secluded estate in a remote corner of Northern Ireland. Many writers have called him a "recluse." His affectionate and devoted biographer, Wilton J. Oldham, takes exception to the term, but it is really a matter of semantics.

After the *Titanic* Ismay never participated in public functions. He never attended Mrs. Ismay's frequent bridge parties and dances. He never traveled to America again. He amused himself sitting on a park bench, chatting anonymously with down-and-outers. He liked to watch passing parades, looking at them alone and lost in the crowd. He died of a stroke at his home in London, October 17, 1937.

Legends about him lived on. In November 1955, shortly after *A Night to Remember* was published, a letter arrived from a racing fan in Britain describing the remarkable finish of the 1913 Derby at Epsom Downs. Craganour, the favorite, crossed the line first and was escorted to the winner's circle. Then, without a protest from the owner or jockey of any other horse in the race, he was suddenly disqualified by the stewards, acting on their own. They awarded the race instead to second-place Aboyeur, a 100-to-1 shot, which they claimed had been bumped by Craganour in the home stretch. Most of the crowd saw no such bumping, and a photograph of the finish shows Aboyeur leaning on Craganour, rather than the other way around. Craganour, my correspondent pointed out, was owned by Bruce Ismay, and the inference was clear: the English racing establishment would never let a horse owned by Ismay win the hallowed Derby.

This was a story worth checking. Everything turned out to be exactly as related, except for one important detail. Craganour was not owned by Bruce Ismay. The owner was Bower Ismay, Bruce's younger brother. Unless the supposed stigma was so great that it affected the whole family, there seems no reason to suppose that Craganour's disqualification had anything to do with the *Titanic*.

In fact, there were other more plausible reasons which might have accounted for the stewards' unprecedented act. Craganour's English jockey had been replaced at the last minute by Johnny Reiff, an American rider imported from France. It was an immensely unpopular switch, and when the stewards interviewed some of the other jockeys in the race before announcing their decision, it was an ideal opportunity to discredit Reiff. But the story will not die; letters still drift in, inseparably linking Craganour and Bruce Ismay together.

Ismay's most vocal American defender was First Class passenger Billy Carter of Philadelphia, but this proved a mixed blessing. Carter turned out to be the only other male passenger in Collapsible C.

There were raised eyebrows about him too, and speculation increased when Mrs. Carter sued for divorce in January 1914. Every effort was made to keep the details secret, but it was rumored that the *Titanic* played a part in the case.

Then, on January 21, 1915, somebody—no one is sure who—released Mrs. Carter's testimony. The grounds for her suit were "cruel and barbarous treatment and indignities to the person," and one passage in particular caught the public's eye:

> When the *Titanic* struck, my husband came to our stateroom and said, "Get up and dress yourself and the children." I never saw him again until I arrived at the *Carpathia* at 8 o'clock the next morning, when I saw him leaning on the rail. All he said was that he had had a jolly good breakfast, and that he never thought I would make it.

Carter denied all charges, stressing that he had had his wife and children placed in one of the boats before he and Ismay jumped into Collapsible C to help with the rowing. A shadow of doubt hovers over this version, since the British Inquiry established that Collapsible C left the *Titanic* some 15 minutes before Mrs. Carter and the children went in Boat 4.

After the divorce, Mrs. Carter married George Brooke, and lived a happily uneventful life until she died in 1934. Billy Carter, vaguely described at the time of the disaster as a polo player and clubman, continued playing polo and going to his clubs, ultimately dying in Palm Beach in 1940.

William T. Sloper of New Britain, Connecticut, was another First Class survivor who had some explaining to do. On April 19, the day after the *Carpathia* reached port, the *New York Journal* identified Sloper as that instant *Titanic* celebrity, "the man who got off dressed as a woman."

Actually, there's no supporting evidence whatsoever. Sloper left the *Titanic* in No. 7, the first boat lowered. At that time few thought the danger was serious, and First Officer Murdoch had difficulty filling the boat at all. Sloper later recalled Murdoch saying, "Any passengers who would like to do so may get into this lifeboat." While it's hard to believe he went that far—"women and children first" was clearly the rule—certainly he let in couples and parties of gentlemen and ladies traveling together. Sloper entered the boat with his companions at bridge that evening: Fred Seward, screen actress Dorothy Gibson, and her mother. Even then, the boat was lowered with only 28 persons—less than half its capacity. For a man to go in Boat 7, there was no reason to dress as a woman.

What, then, was the source of the story? The explanation does not lie in anything that happened on the
decks of the *Titanic*; rather, it can be traced to an incident that happened in the corridors of the Waldorf-
Astoria Hotel the night the *Carpathia* got back to New
York.

Sloper was met at the pier by his brother Harold and
his father, Andrew Jackson Sloper. They whisked him
by taxi to the Waldorf-Astoria, where he was the first
survivor to register. Word quickly spread, and soon the
corridor outside his room was packed with reporters
clamoring for a story. Sloper didn't want to see them,
mainly because he had already scribbled an "exclusive"
for his friend Jack Vance, editor of his hometown paper, the New Britain *Herald*. When Harold Sloper tried
to get rid of the reporters, they made a rush at the door,
which Harold repelled perhaps a little too forcefully. In
any event, the *Journal's* man decided the time had come
to teach the Slopers a little respect for the press: his
story put William Sloper in women's clothing.

For a while Sloper debated whether to sue for libel.
His father counseled against it, arguing that a good lawyer would cost more than any damages he could collect.
Besides, all his real friends knew what had actually happened, and if anyone else preferred to believe some
vindictive reporter, there was nothing anybody could do
about it.

It didn't quite work out that way. William Sloper spent
many an hour in the years ahead explaining how he
really escaped from the *Titanic*. But at least he faced the
matter squarely. Others, too, have been positively identified as "the man who got off dressed as a woman." All

are in the clear, but none fought back, and a cloud hovers over them even today.

Sir Cosmo and Lady Duff Gordon also lived in the shadow of the *Titanic* for the rest of their days. They had left the ship in Boat 1, capacity 40, which pulled away with only 12 people, then failed to heed the cries that went up from the water after the ship sank. It was rumored that Sir Cosmo had bribed the boat crew not to row back.

Lord Mersey exonerated him completely, but did observe that Sir Cosmo might have shown a little more initiative. Instead of doing nothing, he could have led an effort to rescue some of the swimmers.

He just wasn't the type. Naturally reticent, the last thing Sir Cosmo wanted was to be conspicuous. An old Eton boy, he never went to a university, but settled into a quiet life of comfort and privilege. He seemed totally oblivious of the ordinary people around him. It never occurred to him that somebody might misinterpret the £5 gift he presented to each member of his boat crew. (When servants do a good job, you tip them.) Nor did he remotely understand that it might frighten the already jittery survivors when, during the trip back to New York, the boat crew was reassembled in their life jackets for a "team picture." Nor did he have any inkling that it might be in bad taste to have a festive champagne supper at the Ritz after the *Carpathia* landed.

Still, one must carry on. Sir Cosmo became no recluse; he lived the life he had always led—proud, aloof, aware that he was the target of much scorn but never condescending to lower himself to the point of arguing about it. He did not talk much about the *Titanic*, but his wife felt that the storm of censure and ridicule that swirled around him "well-nigh broke his heart." He died in April 1931.

Lucy, Lady Duff Gordon, was a very different case. A high-priced dress designer, she had scrapped her way to the peak of the intensely competitive fashion industry. On top of that she had landed Sir Cosmo, and now she wasn't about to give up any of the ground gained. She met her critics with bravado, almost defiance. What about the £5 that Sir Cosmo gave each member of the boat crew? Her answer was easy: the other *Titanic* passengers should have been as generous.

She remained peppery to the end. By 1934 her business had fallen apart, and she was a faded old lady confined to a tiny house on Hampstead Heath. But when a New York correspondent, seeking an anniversary story, asked her if she had any regrets about the *Titanic*, she shot back: "Regrets? I have no regrets. The *Titanic* disaster made me and my fortune. Look at the tremendous amount of publicity it gave me. . . . When I opened my dress establishments in New York and Chicago, people mobbed the places. I made thousands and thousands of dollars."

She did indeed make a lot of money, but it had nothing to do with the *Titanic*. World War I had closed the great couturier houses of Paris, and wartime austerity had overtaken London. The only people left with spendable money were the rich Americans, and they had no place to spend it. Lady Duff Gordon had the good sense to see this, and opened up new outlets in New York and Chicago. She prospered greatly for a while, but by the end of the war nobody had the kind of money her designs required (one of her dresses used 30 yards of silk at the hem), and the slim, boyish look of the 20's spelled bankruptcy. Broke, but still defiant on the subject of the *Titanic,* she died in April 1935.

For Mrs. Henry B. Harris, the disaster led to a whole new life. "Henry B.," as she always called her lost husband, had been one of Broadway's most successful producers. But the money was current income, not the settled wealth of the Astors or Wideners. When he died, the dollars stopped. Hence her $1,000,000 claim for the loss of his "services." When this was whittled down to $50,000, her prospects looked bleak, since it was generally understood that women had no place in the business end of the theater.

But why not? Henry B. had often depended on her quick, intuitive mind. Moreover, she already had a theater—the choice Hudson on West 43rd Street. So she blazed a trail and became Broadway's first woman producer.

She did very well at it too, backing good plays while developing such stars as Ina Claire and Charles Coburn. She also discovered the playwright Moss Hart and produced his first play, *The Beloved Bandit.* In his autobiography *Act One,* Hart painted a memorable picture of Renée Harris as an unquenchable optimist in the face of first-night disaster.

In World War I she turned her energies to the cause, and did yeoman service staging entertainments for the doughboys in France. General Pershing sent her a personal note of thanks, and she delightedly put it on her wall, where it hung incongruously with the more gushy tributes of other theater people.

The 20's were all velvet. As the money rolled in, she picked up an apartment overlooking Central Park . . . a house in Florida . . . a camp in Maine . . . a yacht . . . and four more husbands. The latter were all just dalliances, she always insisted. Henry B. remained the only man who meant anything, and, in fact, she used the surname "Harris" for the rest of her life.

In 1929 she set off on a leisurely trip around the world . . . and then the roof fell in. The stock market crashed in October, and Renée Harris's fortune vanished even faster than it had materialized. She hurried home, but it was too late. Everything, including the Hudson Theater, was gone. The last of her collection of antiques were auctioned off in 1931.

By 1940 she was reduced to a single room in a welfare hotel. There was nothing left except her sunny disposition. But this never failed her, and was her most striking characteristic when I interviewed her at the time of *A Night to Remember*.

Seeking to find some happy reminder of the old days, I once brought her a little jar of caviar. After one taste she gently pushed it aside. I took this as a challenge and from time to time tried again. Always her response was the same: "You call *that* caviar?" she would ask with cheerful incredulity.

She liked to talk about the *Titanic*, and her shrewd theatrical eye caught all sorts of nuances. Poor as a church mouse but radiantly blissful, she died quietly in September 1969 at the age of 93.

Helen Churchill Candee was another *Titanic* survivor who managed to cope with adversity. "Our coterie," as Colonel Gracie called her little circle of shipboard swains, was forever shattered: Colley, Kent, and Clinch Smith drowned; Gracie died from the aftereffects within nine months; only Hugh Woolner and Bjornstrom Steffanson survived. As far as can be determined, she was never again in touch with either of them.

Putting the past behind her, Mrs. Candee turned to the galleys of her new book on tapestry. Titled simply *The Tapestry Book,* it was published in 1913, receiving a fine review in the *Times.* During the 20's she carved out a whole new career as a travel lecturer on exotic places. China and Southeast Asia were her specialties, and her book *Angkor, the Magnificent* earned her decorations from both the French government and the King of Cambodia. Nor did she just stick to sightseeing. As early as 1927 she was warning her listeners of the rising tide of anticolonialism in the area.

Through it all, she continued to charm everyone she met. She remained active until just before her death at the age of 90 in her summer home at York Harbor, Maine.

Many of the *Titanic* widows soon married again—another sign that the Victorian Age was over, with its interminable years of mourning and dripping black veils. Besides Renée Harris, the list included prominent names like Mrs. Astor, Mrs. Widener, and (a little later) Mrs. Ryerson. Among this group Mrs. Lucien P. Smith deserves special note. Her new husband was Robert Daniel, a fellow survivor whom she met on the *Carpathia.* The tennis player Karl Behr also married a survivor, but in his case it was no chance meeting. He had pursued Helen Newsom across the Atlantic and back.

Most survivors picked up pretty much where they left

off, and one was back in business even before he reached dry land. Cardsharp and confidence man George Brayton had been in the *Titanic*'s smoking room stalking a prospective victim when the ship struck. He escaped in one of the starboard boats, and by the time the *Carpathia* docked in New York, he had already met and picked out a new pigeon.

Henry C. E. Stengel was a Newark, New Jersey, leather manufacturer, one of the two other passengers who had been in Boat 1 with the Duff Gordon party. Strolling the *Carpathia*'s deck on the second day after rescue, he noticed a man looking downcast, and politely inquired what was the matter. The man, who turned out to be George Brayton, explained that he had to get to Los Angeles but had lost all his money. Stengel advised him to ask the White Star Line to advance him his fare.

Nothing more was said at the moment, but shortly after the *Carpathia* landed, Stengel received a phone call from Brayton reporting that White Star had come through, that he would be leaving soon for Los Angeles, and that he just wanted to thank Stengel for his interest. Pleased, Stengel asked Brayton to dinner at his home in Newark that night.

During the evening Brayton mentioned a big deal pending in New York, which would come to a head as soon as his brother-in-law, an executive with Western Union, got back from a trip to Mexico. Several weeks later Stengel received another phone call from Brayton, reporting that the brother-in-law was back and in a position to make some money. He'd like to cut Stengel in on the deal.

Stengel hurried to New York, where he, Brayton, and

the brother-in-law ended up in a room at the Hotel Seville. Here the brother-in-law explained that he was in charge of the "RD" Department at Western Union. This was the department responsible for flashing the results of horse races, and he was in a position to withhold the results for at least eight minutes—allowing a wonderful opportunity to bet on a sure thing. It would cost Stengel just $1,000 to get in on the scheme.

Stengel later said that at this point he sailed into the brother-in-law, and when Brayton pleaded with him not to "squeal," Stengel began punching him too. Finally, the scuffle ended, but by the time the police were called, the con men had slipped away.

George Brayton fades from the *Titanic* story at this point. With his collection of aliases, his deft moves, and his instinct for survival, it seems safe to assume that under some other name he continued plying his trade on the North Atlantic run.

Finally, what about the *Titanic*'s surviving officers? In view of their splendid discipline that last night—and their loyalty to White Star on the witness stand—one might suppose they enjoyed steady promotion, crowned by a command as their just reward.

It didn't work out that way. No officer from the *Titanic* ever achieved his own command, no matter how brave or loyal he may have been. The White Star Line was determined to take no step that might remind the traveling public of its darkest hour.

Fifth Officer Lowe was appointed Third Officer on the *Medic,* a minor vessel on the Australian run—obviously a dead end. He served in the Royal Navy during the First World War, then retired to his native Wales.

Fourth Officer Boxhall hung on through the merger of White Star and Cunard, but advancement in the 30's was painfully slow. He finally retired as Chief Officer of the small Cunarder *Ausonia*. Third Officer Pitman decided his eyes weren't good enough for a deck officer, shifted to the Purser's Section, and spent the rest of his seagoing days shuffling paper.

Second Officer Lightoller also served in the Royal Navy during the first war. He returned to White Star after the Armistice and was made Chief Officer of the lumbering *Celtic*. For a while he had hopes of a transfer to the crack *Olympic*, but was passed over. He retired from the sea in the early 20's and tried his hand (not too successfully) at everything from writing columns to raising chickens.

But the sea still ran in his blood. He designed and sailed his own yacht *Sundowner* and had a final taste of peril in 1940. He took *Sundowner* over to Dunkirk with the great fleet of "little ships," and rescued 131 British soldiers. At his best in the midst of disaster, he cheerfully wrote a friend several days later, "We've got our tails well up and are going to win no matter when or how."

CHAPTER XVII

Unlocking the Ocean's Secret

"**S**he's gone; that's the last of her," someone sighed in Boat 13 as the sea closed over the flagstaff on the *Titanic*'s stern. Actually, it was anything but the last of her. Figuratively, she would always be afloat, gripping the world's imagination for years to come. Literally, she would be seen again 73 years later, thanks to the miracle of modern technology.

Men began dreaming up ways to find and raise the *Titanic* right from the start. In March 1914—less than two years after the disaster—a Denver architect named Charles Smith published a plan based on the use of electromagnets. These would be attached to a specially designed submarine, which would dive down from the *Titanic*'s radioed position, 41°46′N, 50°14′W. The steel hull of the liner would immediately attract the magnets, drawing the sub to the sunken vessel's side. With the exact location of the ship now fixed, more electromagnets would be sent down and attached directly to her hull. Cables would run from these magnets to winches on a fleet of barges stationed above the wreck. At a given signal, the winches would all be wound up, pulling the *Titanic* to the surface.

Mr. Smith's plan had a precise quality that was quite enticing. Surely, any inventor must have done his homework who said he would need exactly 162 men—no more, no less. But Smith also said he would need $1.5 million, and it was here that his scheme met a fate that would become all too familiar: nobody would put up the money.

Electromagnetism had much popular appeal in these primitive days before "high tech." Another plan, which apparently never got farther than the Sunday-supplement pages, called for magnets to be fastened to the sunken *Titanic* and attached by cable to empty pontoons, rising above the hulk like a cluster of circus balloons. When enough pontoons had been added, presumably the ship would come popping up.

Two world wars, the carefree 20's, and the depression 30's put a temporary end to such schemes. No one had the time or inclination to dive on the *Titanic*. Not enough years had passed for legends to sprout about the supposed great treasure aboard the ship (some said diamonds, others gold), and perhaps most important, the "fascination factor" was low. Finding the *Titanic* would ultimately become a challenge like scaling Mount Everest—because it is there—but not yet.

The 50's saw the first flicker of renewed interest. In July 1953 the British salvage vessel *Help,* on charter from the Admiralty to the salvage firm Risdon Beazley Ltd., slipped quietly out of Southampton Harbor and headed for the *Titanic*'s position. Here the *Help* began underwater blasting with heavy explosives. No one would say what she was up to, but she was equipped with deep-set telephoto cameras and remotely controlled retrieval gear. It seems likely that the operators hoped to blow open the *Titanic*'s hull and search for some of the treasure rumored to be inside.

Nothing was found—not even a trace of the ship—but the *Help* was back next summer for another try. Again, nothing turned up, and this time Risdon Beazley Ltd. had enough. They vanish from the story.

The 60's brought a dramatic surge of activity. It was a time of great technological advances. Men conquered space—even went to the moon—and there was a parallel, if less spectacular, leap forward in oceanography and our ability to explore the world beneath the sea. At the same time, the triumph of the jet plane as the norm in trans-Atlantic travel focused attention on that suddenly "endangered species," the ocean liner . . . and this of course included the *Titanic*. Even the political and social climates seemed to contribute. It was a time of questioning values, and what could be more fascinating than peering closely at the symbols of a period when everyone seemed to know their place? The *Titanic* became an intriguing artifact of the smug little Edwardian world.

None of this was especially surprising. What *was* surprising was the particular individual who led the parade. Douglas Woolley knew nothing about oceanography. He was an English workman who dyed nylon stockings in a hosiery factory. He had no scientific training, no experience in salvage, no college degree, no financial resources; but he did have an obsession about the *Titanic*. Sitting in his cluttered one-room flat in the small English town of Baldock, he whiled away the hours

dreaming of finding and raising the lost liner. He also
had a remarkable knack of getting his plans into the
newspapers. Apparently, through some intuitive understanding of an editor's mind, he could regularly get cov-
erage that would be the envy of a highly paid public
relations consultant.

Starting in 1966, Woolley announced his plans for
raising the *Titanic* almost annually, and every time the
press would pick up his release and give it fresh treatment, as though it had never happened before. At first
he made only the local papers, but by 1968 he was appearing in even the august *Times*.

As reported in the press, Woolley originally planned
to find the *Titanic* by means of a "bathyscaphe," and
then raise her by means of nylon balloons attached to
her hull. These would be pumped full of air, letting the
ship "gently rise to the surface." How the balloons would
be inflated 13,000 feet down wasn't clear.

For a while it seemed as if something might actually
come of Woolley's dreams. Two Hungarian inventors
turned up with a plan that looked, on paper at least,
impressively scientific. An admittedly shadowy group of
West German investors (some said three; others, ten)
promised the necessary capital. A London accountant
incorporated the project as the *Titanic* Salvage Company. And finally, even a boat was obtained, which
Woolley thought could be turned into a practical salvage
vessel.

Then all began to unravel. The Hungarians' plan
called for plastic bags to be filled with hydrogen produced by electrolysis of the seawater, and only a week
had been allowed to generate the 85,000 cubic yards of
hydrogen that would theoretically be needed to move

the *Titanic*. A scholarly paper by an American chemistry professor showed that it might take not a week, but ten years. The West German investors never materialized; the *Titanic* Salvage Company remained little more than a name; and even the boat turned out to be a dud. Lying at Newlyn in Cornwall, it was so old and rusty that local fishermen predicted it would never get out of the harbor. Gradually the whole project evaporated.

But Douglas Woolley did achieve one thing. He started a lot more people thinking about finding the *Titanic*. During the 1970's at least eight different groups planned to explore the ship. Some wanted only to locate and film her; others hoped to raise her, and there was no limit to their ingenuity. One plan called for 180,000 tons of molten wax to be pumped into the vessel. When hardened, the wax would become buoyant and lift the *Titanic* to the surface. Another plan would work the same way, but with Vaseline.

Still another plan would achieve buoyancy by injecting thousands of Ping-Pong balls into the hull. Another would employ gigantic winches to crank the ship up. Yet another would encase the liner in ice. Then, like an ordinary cube in a drink, the ice would rise to the surface, bringing the *Titanic* with it.

Whatever the practicality, all the plans suffered from a common fault: they cost too much. One scheme, for instance, contemplated the use of benthos glass floats . . . but it turned out that the necessary number would cost $238,214,265.

Just mounting the expedition would require more than most people were willing to risk. A truly suitable vessel—and there were very few—would eat up $10,000 a day. Add to this the cost of the equipment needed, which looked like a list drawn up on another planet: a deep-tow wide-screen sonar sled, a three-axis magnetometer, a sub-bottom profiler, a depressor, and a number of acoustic transponders . . . plus a payroll that covered every requirement from a top oceanographer to a decent cook. Altogether, the total outlay could easily run over a million dollars.

Nor was it a sure thing even then. The exact position of the *Titanic* remained uncertain, and the search required a calm sea in one of the roughest areas of ocean in the world. No wonder the odds-makers put the chances of finding the ship at less than 50% to 60%.

These odds were good enough for Jack Grimm, a wealthy Texas wildcat oilman, who appeared on the scene in 1980. He had already sponsored expeditions in search of Noah's ark, the Loch Ness monster, and the legendary Big Foot. Now, when a professional expedition leader named Mike Harris suggested the *Titanic* as a new project, Grimm quickly agreed. After all, he had drilled 25 straight dry holes before he finally hit his first gusher. Compared to striking oil, the chances of finding the *Titanic* seemed almost promising. Moreover, there were the dividends: fame, publicity, adventure.

Jack Grimm gave it his best shot. He talked up the project at the Petroleum Club in his hometown, Abilene, got some of his poker-playing buddies to take a piece of the action. He hired the William Morris Agency to handle TV, movie, and serialization rights. He arranged for a book. He persuaded Orson Welles to narrate a documentary.

Above all, he won respectability. In a deal with Columbia University, Grimm gave $330,000 to the Lamont-Doherty Geological Observatory for a wide-sweep sonar rig, and in return got five years' exclusive use of the equipment plus the services of the technical personnel needed to run it. Lured by the prospects, two distinguished oceanographers also signed on: Dr. William Ryan of Columbia and Dr. Fred Spiess of the Scripps Institution in California.

July 17, 1980, the expedition set out from Port Everglades, Florida, in the research vessel *H.J.W. Fay.* They reached the search area on the 29th, and for the next three weeks plodded back and forth with no really promising results. Finally, they ran out of time and went back home.

June 29, 1981, they headed out again, this time on the research vessel *Gyre.* Reaching the search area, they spent nine days checking out possibilities suggested by their sonar the previous summer, and scanning other less likely areas. Again nothing definite, although Grimm felt sure they had located a propeller.

July 1983, they returned for one more try, now on the research vessel *Robert Conrad.* This time the cameras didn't function properly, and they were further handicapped by high seas. After two weeks they again returned home empty-handed. An optimist in the ship's company felt that the sonar had picked up a profile characteristic of the *Titanic,* but the world remained unconvinced. One skeptic thought that it looked more like "a computer code on a can of green beans."

Aware of these fruitless efforts, the press paid little attention when still another group set out to find the *Titanic* in the summer of 1985. This time the sponsor was the Woods Hole Oceanographic Institution; the ship was the Institution's 245-foot research vessel *Knorr;* and the leader was Dr. Robert D. Ballard, a personable 42-year-old geologist, who headed up the Institution's Deep Submergence Laboratory. To the casual observer, the expedition appeared to be like all the others—an ungainly-looking boat loaded with mysterious hardware.

First, a stop at the Azores. Here Bob Ballard and most of his team joined the ship. There were now a total of 49 people aboard—24 scientists and 25 in the crew. Leaving Ponta Delgada on August 15, they headed not northwest for the *Titanic*, but southeast for the position of the U.S. nuclear submarine *Scorpion*, mysteriously lost with all hands in 1968. They spent the 17th taking pictures of the sunken sub, and if these photographs throw any new light on what happened to her, this could well be the most important accomplishment of the entire expedition. At the time, it went virtually unnoticed.

Then on to the search area, a 150-square-mile block of sea based on the *Titanic*'s last given position. Some 80% of this area had been combed earlier in the summer by the French government's research vessel, *Le Suroit*. She had not found anything, but her presence pointed up the fact that the expedition was a joint Franco-American venture, manned by scientists from both countries. The main American contribution was a unique video camera system built into a deep-towed vehicle called *Argo*; while the French contributed a revolutionary side-scanning sonar named SAR, which could examine the ocean floor in swaths three fifths of a mile wide—far beyond the limits of anything previously invented.

In keeping with the partnership concept, Bob Ballard had been on *Le Suroit* during July, working with her team of scientists. They had spent six weeks "mowing the lawn" (as the oceanographers put it) until *Le Suroit* finally ran out of time and had to go home. Now Jean Jarry, director of the French effort, was serving on the *Knorr* with two of his group.

Arriving on the scene August 22, the *Knorr* took over where *Le Suroit* left off. Behind her, and nearly 13,000 feet down, she towed *Argo*. Roughly the size of an automobile, it carried the newly devised video system. No less than five television cameras (pointing ahead, downward, and sideways) were packed into the unit, along with sonar, sensors, computerized timing equipment, and banks of powerful strobe lights. Overall, the contraption was virtually a robot, managed by scientists over two miles above, sitting in the relative comfort of the *Knorr*'s control room.

But even *Argo* didn't seem able to conjure up the *Titanic*. Day after day slipped by, and the men monitoring the screens in the control room saw only the same empty seabed. Occasionally a rat-tailed fish might swim briefly into view, but for the most part it was just mile after mile of mud and sand dunes.

The night of August 31–September 1 began like all the others. The *Knorr* crept slowly along the path of the search pattern, deep-towing *Argo* as usual. In the control room a seven-man watch under Bob Ballard dutifully monitored the video screens, but there was nothing interesting to look at—just more miles of mud. At midnight Ballard's group was relieved by the 12:00 to 4:00 watch under Jean-Louis Michel, leader of the French scientists. Ballard went below for a shower and some rest.

Shortly before 1:00, small chunks of metal debris suddenly began showing up on the screens. They were unidentifiable, but definitely not part of the natural seascape.

"You'd better go and get Bob," Michel ordered, but the group in the control room seemed riveted to the spot, fascinated by the fast-growing trail of debris. Finally, someone persuaded the cook to go, and he brought back Ballard in time to see a large metal cylinder appear on the video tube at 1:05.

It was clearly a boiler. Better than that, it was unmistakably a boiler from the *Titanic*. Nothing else could have that particular arrangement of three stoking doors at one end, or that particular configuration of rivets. Ballard's team had studied pictures of those boilers for months—knew them by heart—and now they had found one.

It was only the beginning. The scientists estimated that the debris trail ran for nearly 600 yards, with a huge, shadowy, solid object at the end. But they would not find out what it was tonight. Twenty minutes had passed since the filming of the debris began, and it was now so thick that Ballard feared *Argo* might become entangled in some piece of rigging and be damaged or lost. Playing it safe, he ordered the unit to be hauled up until the bottom could be more thoroughly checked by sonar.

At 1:40 someone observed that it was close to the time of night when the *Titanic* made her final plunge. The remark gave Ballard an idea. He had always been deeply aware of the immense tragedy that lay behind this expedition; now he invited the group to join him on the fantail for a brief memorial service.

Next morning the sonar check indicated that it was safe for *Argo* to go back to work, and it soon became clear that the huge shadowy object at the end of the debris trail was the forepart of the *Titanic* herself. She was in astonishingly good shape. When last seen that April night in 1912, the ship was plunging head first almost straight down, but somehow she had leveled off and landed gently on the bottom. Now she sat upright, with just a slight list to port. The forecastle was not crumpled, and even the anchor chains were neatly aligned, as though ready for one of Captain Smith's Sunday inspections.

Most amazing of all was the *Titanic*'s pristine appearance. There was little of the marine growth that usually sprouts all over a sunken vessel. At 13,000 feet it was too dark and too cold for anything to grow. Only a thin film of silt covered the ship—so thin that it was easy to count every rivet and trace the lines of every plank in her decks.

The clarity was so great that dozens of objects could be identified amid the debris alongside the ship: lumps of coal . . . luggage . . . beds . . . bottles of wine miraculously unbroken . . . a silver platter . . . a chamberpot. The sharpness of detail gave the disaster an immediacy that sobered even the excitement of discovery.

For the next five days the *Knorr* cruised back and forth over the *Titanic*'s grave, deep-towing *Argo* behind her. *Argo* videotaped the wreck from every angle, and later another deep-towed robot named *Angus* made a series of passes using cameras loaded with 35-mm. color film. They covered most of the forward end of the ship, and far enough aft to learn that the stern was missing. Pictures taken by *Angus* on the fifth day caught debris from the missing section about 800 feet aft of the rest of the wreck. The first and last funnels were gone too, and *Argo* had a narrow escape when it brushed against the second funnel while making a turn.

Perhaps Ballard felt at this point that he had stretched his luck enough. The rest could wait until next year, when he planned to return with a manned submersible named *Alvin*. In any case, September 5 was the last day of filming. The *Knorr* turned for Woods Hole and a noisy welcome of Klaxons and air horns.

Why did this effort succeed when all the others failed? First of all, there was the equipment. It was not that the other expeditions cut corners; technology was simply moving so fast that Ballard enjoyed an extra edge. *Argo*'s side-scanning sonar, for instance, could cover as much ground in 20 days as previously took 12 years.

Money was another factor. Even a wealthy Texan couldn't match the combined resources of the French government, the U.S. Navy, the National Science Foundation, and the National Geographic Society. The Office of Naval Research sank $2.8 million into *Argo* alone. Altogether, it's estimated that the expedition cost $6 million, with a possible total of $15 million if certain projected equipment was added.

Another advantage was Ballard's team of assistants. Most were "old pros," and Emory Kristof, a staff photographer with the *National Geographic* magazine, had worked with Ballard for years developing new techniques in underwater photography, always with the *Titanic* in mind.

Finally there was Ballard himself. He not only had a Ph.D. in marine geology and geophysics plus a fistful of scientific awards; he was also a diver with much practical experience in deep-sea submersibles. And he had been hooked on the *Titanic* for years. As early as 1978, according to an article appearing that year in *The Washington Post*, he was president of Seaonics International Ltd., "a firm formed with the express purpose of finding the *Titanic*." His almost passionate interest makes odd reading of the accounts in *The New York Times* and elsewhere, stating that the *Titanic* was a "surprise yield" of sea trials conducted to test new underwater research equipment.

Add to these assets the intuition that seems to guide successful inventors and explorers. As one colleague put it: "Bob has an extraordinary ability to find interesting things on the bottom."

But his most striking quality was a sensitivity that verged on piety. It was there the night the *Titanic* was found and he held that brief service on the *Knorr*'s fantail. It was there in his frequent references to the lost "souls" below. And it was there at the press conference in Washington after the *Knorr*'s return. Even the hardest cases were moved by the closing lines of his formal statement:

> The *Titanic* itself lies in 13,000 feet of water on a gently sloping alpine-like countryside overlooking a small canyon below.
>
> Its bow faces north and the ship sits upright on the bottom. Its mighty stacks pointing upward.
>
> There is no light at this great depth and little light can be found.
>
> It is quiet and peaceful and a fitting place for the remains of this greatest of sea tragedies to rest.
>
> May it forever remain that way and may God bless these found souls.

A noble thought, but "forever" is a long, long while. Pompeii was once the scene of an enormous human tragedy, but now it is a fascinating dig. King

Tutankhamen's tomb was a sacred grave, but today it's a tourist attraction. The same sort of fate must ultimately overtake the *Titanic,* and meanwhile who is to police the site? A resolution passed by the House of Representatives urges that the wreck be designated a maritime memorial, protected by international treaty, but the sea belongs to no one, and there are few funds for guarding a patch of ocean.

The danger lies not in man's greed but in his curiosity. By now nearly everyone knows that no great treasure is tucked away somewhere in the *Titanic.* There is no evidence of a fortune in diamonds or gold. Her cargo manifest lists ordinary goods worth less than $500,000; the passengers' jewelry was impressive but not spectacular. Mrs. Widener's fabulous pearls were saved. Nor is there any practical chance of raising the *Titanic* for commercial purposes.

But the lure of the ship remains, if only because "it is there." Again, she is like Mount Everest. As new technology makes the *Titanic* ever more accessible, all that is left to protect her is a human sense of propriety. A congressional resolution designating the wreck as a "maritime memorial" is not enough.

Maybe it doesn't really matter. Those who fall under the spell of that famous night will always have their own favorite vignette as a special memorial—perhaps the band, or the Strauses, or the eight Goodwins clinging together. And there will always be the memory of that last glimpse of the *Titanic* as she stood in 1912—stern high; her black silhouette pointing like an accusing finger at the stars; then gliding slowly out of sight, leaving her handful of lifeboats alone in the empty sea.

Gleanings from the Testimony

It is impossible to be very knowledgeable about the *Titanic* without studying the official records of the American and British investigations. This is no easy task. There are 181 witnesses and 2,111 pages of testimony. Some of it is ambiguous, inconsistent, and even contradictory.

Here is an attempt to sift the opinions of various witnesses on several of the more controversial points. After each witness's name, source is indicated by page number in the Senate hearings and by question number in the British proceedings. These gleanings may prove useful, if only because they show how hard it is to corner that elusive quarry, the truth. . . .

Weather at time of collision

"Perfectly clear . . . you could almost see the stars set." (Boxhall, US 224, 231, 256) "Perfectly clear" (Boxhall, Br 15338-15340)

Very clear ... "we could see the stars setting." (Lightoller, US 68). Perfectly clear and fine (Lightoller, Br 13523, 13528, 14194, 14196)

Fine night (Rowe, Br 17602)

"There was a haze right ahead ... a haze on the water." (Lee, Br 2401-2408)

Haze "nothing to talk about" (Fleet, Br 17253, 17266-17268, 17271, 17253, 17390, 17393)

Clear, starlit (Hitchens, Br 1191)

"We could not have wished for better weather." (Lucas, Br 1405)

"Grand" (Poingdestre, Br 2780)

Haze (Shivers, Br 4700)

"A very clear night" (Symons, Br 11984)

"A beautiful night . . . a dark night, but starlight" (Peuchen, US 350)

The iceberg

Round and had one big point sticking up on one side of it, about 100' high. (Osman, US 539)

When first sighted, berg looked about as large as two tables put together, but kept getting larger as ship approached. When alongside, a little higher than forecastle head, which is about 50' above water (Fleet, US 320). . . . Just a little bit higher than the forecastle head, but not as high as the crow's nest (Fleet, Br 17277, 17304-14)

Berg roughly 100' high (Rowe, US 521)

Looked like Rock of Gibraltar from Europe Point, "only much smaller." (Scarrott, Br 361-362)

Looked like a large black object, "much higher" than B Deck. (Crawford, US 842-843)

Berg about the height of the Boat Deck; if anything just a little higher. Top was pointed. (Olliver, US 527)

Higher than the forecastle (Lee, Br 2439)

Movements of ship after collision

—In engine room. Immediately after collision engine room telegraph signaled "STOP" . . . 10–15 minutes, then "slow ahead" . . . 10 minutes, then "STOP" . . . 4–5 minutes, then "slow astern" . . . 5 minutes, then "STOP." "I do not think the telegraph went after that." (Scott, Br 5609-5626, 5807-5809, 5836)

—Coming on bridge right after collision, heard orders given to put helm hard aport. By this time iceberg astern. Shortly afterward Captain telegraphed half-speed ahead. Doesn't know whether engines were stopped or astern at time, but ship "almost stopped" when he did it. (Olliver, US 527-528, 531-532)

—On bridge. Murdoch to Smith immediately after collision: "I put hard astarboard and ran the engines full astern, but it was too close; she hit it . . . I intended to port around it, but she hit before I could do any more." On reaching bridge right after impact, notices engine room telegraphs indicate "Full speed astern." (Boxhall, US 229-230; Br 15346-15355, 15505)

—On deck immediately after collision. Berg abaft the starboard beam, less than ship's length away. Ship seemed to be under port helm, stern slewing off berg, now going to starboard around it. (Scarrott, Br 351-356)

—In Boiler Room 6. Immediately after crash, telegraph went to "STOP." Orders passed, "Shut the dampers." Then watertight doors dropped. Doors closed "less than 5 minutes" after bridge signaled to stop engines. (Beauchamp, Br 664-668A)

—On bridge. Just before ship struck, ordered to put helm "hard astarboard." Turned wheel and ship had swung about two points when she struck. At same time order hard astarboard given, Murdoch signals engine room, presumably "Stop. Full speed astern." Ship never under port helm. (Hitchens, Br 948-993, 1314-1316) Ordered to put the helm "hard astarboard." Does so immediately, with crash coming almost at same time. Only order given before collision (Hitchens, US 450, 456)

—First Class stateroom. Impact. Then engines stop. Two or 3 minutes, and then they start again, but very slightly. (Stengel, US 974-975)

—In electric workshop, E Deck. Feels slight jar ... 2 minutes later looks around and sees turbine engine has stopped. (Ranger, Br 3997-4002)

—In Boiler Room 6. Signal light flashed red, meaning stop. Calls to shut the dampers. Then crash, before all dampers shut (Barrett, Br 1860-1867)

—In engine room. Telegraph rang shortly before crash—maybe 2 seconds—then crash and about a minute and a half later engines stopped. Another half-minute and engines go slow astern. Go slow astern about 2 minutes, then stop again. Then ahead for about 2 minutes, then stop for good. Watertight doors closed about 3 minutes after collision. (Dillon, Br 3715-3729, 3736)

—Steward's quarters. Awakened by stopping of engines. Felt no shock before that. Then felt engines going full speed astern and at same time heard warning bells for watertight doors. (Rule, Br 9752-9760)

Light seen from the *Titanic*

Nothing sighted from crow's nest before collision. (Lee, Br 2419-2420; Fleet, US 328, 358)

Moving. First sighted shortly after collision, just as men beginning to turn out the boats. Went to bridge and took a look before going to wireless room with position. Saw "a four-masted steamer" almost dead ahead, 5 or 6 miles. Seemed to be approaching; saw mast lights, then red side light. Later seemed to turn around "very, very slowly" and head away. (Boxhall, US 235-236, 909-910; Br 15385-15409)

First sighted "when we were turning out the boats." (Buley, US 612)

Saw only one light, that while getting the boats out, two points off the port bow. (Lightoller, US 448-449)

Lay to north and *Titanic* pointed east at the time Boat 6 was lowered. (Peuchen US 346)

A single light, off the port bow while boats were being loaded. Thinks it may have been 6 miles. (Gracie, US 990)

To the north (Hart, Br 10268)

Apparently to north. *Titanic's* stern was swinging south, making bow face north, and light was half a point on port bow, about 5 miles away. (Rowe, Br 17669-17674)

Apparently to north, judging from Boat 3's experiences with ice (Moore, US 564)

Apparently to the north—No. 8 had to "turn around" to go to *Carpathia*. (Crawford, US 827; Br 18002, 18087; Jones, US 570) . . . So did No. 11 (Wheelton, US 544) . . . So did No. 16 (Archer, US 648) . . . So did Collapsible C (Rowe, US 520)

Two masthead lights bearing north on starboard bow (Hart, Br 10264-74)

Saw faint red side light and steaming light abeam starboard side of ship—8 or 9 miles off, "right on horizon." But did not see it until after Collapsible D was launched. "Light went farther away every time we looked at it." (Lucas, Br 1566-1585, 1800-1806)

Stationary (Rowe, US 524; Pitman, US 295, 307; Crawford, US 827, 828; Buley, US 611, 612; Fleet, US 358-359; Lightoller, Br 14149)

There all night. As seen from Boat 3 (Moore, US 565). . . . From Boat 6 (Fleet, US 359). . . . From Boat 8 (Jones, US 570; Crawford, US 114, 827, 828; Br 17854, 17856, 17867-69, 17997, 18001-03, 18010, 18017, 18069). . . . From Boat 11 (Wheelton, US 544). . . . From Boat 16 (Archer, US 648). . . .From Collapsible C (Rowe, US 520, 524; Ismay, Br 18577-98)

Suggests light he saw may not have been same light others saw off port bow. (Ismay, Br 18577-98)

Always seemed about same distance away. (Rowe, Br 17666)

No. 11 rows for light "about two hours" (Mackay, Br 10809) . . . pulled for light till daybreak. (Wheelton, US 544)

Collapsible C. Pulled for light till wind sprang up "toward daylight." (Rowe, US 524)

No. 3. "Kept pulling for it until daylight." (Moore, US 565)

Saw it for 20 minutes off the port bow, 8–10 miles away. (Johnson, Br 3482-3486)

Moving. While loading No. 6, saw light 2 points on port bow about 5 miles away. "Surmised it to be a steamboat." Ordered to steer for it, but could get no closer. "Light was moving, gradually disappearing." (Hitchens, Br 1161-1184, 1338-1339) At U.S. Inquiry, said he thought it was a fishing schooner. (Hitchins, Br 1338)

Saw white light on port bow about time No. 6 was being lowered. Definitely a ship, but could not tell whether sail or steamer. (Fleet, Br 17428-35, 17453-56)

Moving. Boat 2 saw light for about an hour. Thought it was a Cape Codder that sailed away. (Osman, US 538)

Looked like a sailing ship. (Bright, US 536)

Single white light point and a half on port bow, 5–10 miles away—couldn't tell what it was—just a vessel—later thought it was a cod-bankman or fishing vessel. (Symons, Br 11468-78)

While readying No. 1, hears a ship has been sighted on port bow, glances over, sees 2 mastheads and red light of a steamer. (Lowe, Br 15825-26)

Before No. 1 lowered, saw bright light "5 or 6 miles ahead of us." Didn't see it after boat lowered. (Hendrickson, Br 11072-11076)

No. 9. Saw red light, then red and white, then red disappears, leaving just white. Thinks it's port light of a steamer 7–8 miles away. Both lights disappear, but 10–15 minutes later sees a white light again, same direction. (Wynn, Br. 13336-51)

Rockets

—Rockets, in general: "Regulations for Preventing Collisions at Sea," Article 31, No. 3, defines distress signals at night: "Rockets or shells, throwing stars of any color or description. . . ." (Hitchens, Br 1199)

—Description of *Titanic*'s rockets (Wilding, Br 20575-20577; Boxhall, Br 15394-15400; Lightoller, Br 14150-14155; 14168-14172)

—Unmistakably signals of distress; not like company signals at all (Lightoller, Br 14150-14155; 14168-14172)

—Discussion of sound (Pitman, US 294; Lightoller, Br 14155)

—About 12:25 Rowe and Bright ordered to bring detonators to bridge for firing distress signals. (Rowe, US 519; Bright, US 832)

—Assisted in firing of rockets from 12:45 to about 1:25. (Rowe, Br 17684)

—Helped fire rockets till about 1:25, then ordered by Captain Smith to stop and help man Collapsible C. (Rowe, US 519)

—Boats 7 and 5 launched before first rockets. (Pitman, US 289, 293, 307)

—First went off between loading of Boats 5 and 3. (Lowe, US 401)

—Rockets began going up as No. 3 lowered (Duff-Gordon, Br 12496). . . . First rocket went off while loading No. 3. (Lowe, US 401)

—Watched them from No. 5. (Pitman, Br 15066; Crosby, US 1145)

—Going off before No. 6 left, and continued half an hour after boat left ship. (Hitchens, Br 1195-1197, 1201, 1207)

—Still going up after Boat 6 launched. (Fleet, US 328)

—Watched from boat 6. (Hitchens, Br 1195-1208)

—Going up after No. 8 pulled away, also Morse lamp. (Crawford, Br 17972)

—Going off while No. 1 cleared and prepared for lowering. (Hendrickson, Br 4997, 5006; Boxhall, US 239)

—Still going up as No. 1 loaded and lowered. Fired one after No. 1 lowered. (Boxhall, US 239)

—While loading No. 1: "Incessantly going off . . . nearly deafening me." (Lowe, US 401)

—Going up before Boat 13 lowered and watched from Boat 13 after afloat. (Lee, Br 2582-2583, 2680)

—Going up as No. 15 left. (Hart, Br 10103)

—Watched from Boat 12. (Poingdestre, Br 3099-3100)

—Continued firing until ordered into Boat 2. (Boxhall, US 237)

—Thinks they were seen by *Californian*. (Ismay, Br 18943-18946)

—Did not hear and did not think he was near enough to hear *Carpathia*'s rockets when he saw them from Collapsible B. (Lightoller, Br 14856)

State of the ship

As Boat 5 pulled away, noticed ship was 15–20 feet down at the bows. (Olliver, US 533)

As No. 1 pulled away, ports under her name just awash. (Symons, Br 11490-11493)

When No. 10 left, water about 10 feet from port "bow light" (Evans, US 753). . . . Port bow light under water when No. 10 lowered. (Buley, US 606)

When No. 13 lowered, forecastle head not under water. (Barrett, Br 2140-2142; Lee, Br 2541-2542)

When No. 2 pulled away, down "by the bridge." (Johnson, Br 3556)

At 1:50 forecastle head close to water. (Jewell, Br 167)

When Collapsible C left, well deck awash but forecastle head not yet submerged. (Rowe, Br 17687-17688)

When No. 4 lowered, A Deck "only about 20 feet from the sea." Could see water washing into open portholes. (Mrs. Ryerson, US 1107)

When "D" lowered, forecastle head just going under water—"that would be about 20 feet lower than the bridge." (Bright, US 839)

When Collapsible D lowered, water right up to bridge. (Lucas, Br 1518, 1528, 1534, 1548)

When "D" lowered, Boat Deck only 10 feet from sea. Water at A Deck. (Lightoller, Br 1420, 14023)

As Boat D lowered, water washes onto A Deck, port side all the way forward. (Woolner, US 887)

Final plunge

As seen from Boat 1. She took a heavy cant, bow down, stern well out of the water. Then, as she went down, her poop righted itself, and he thought, "The poop is going to float." But 2 or 3 minutes later, poop went up "as straight as anything," then "a sound like thunder and soon she disappeared from view."' . . . "Stern righted itself without the bow; in my estimation she must have broken in half . . . about abeam of the after funnel." (Symons, Br 11512-11525, 11722)

Boat 2. "After she got to a certain angle she exploded, broke in halves, and it seemed to me as if all her engines and everything that was in the after part slid out into the forward part, and the after part came up right again, and as soon as it came up, right down it went again." (Osman, US 541)

Boat 3. Saw the forward part go down, then looked as if she broke in half, and then the after part went. (Moore, US 563)

Boat 4. Forward end seemed to break off, after part came back on an even keel, then turned up and went down steadily. (Ranger, Br 4094-4102, 4114, 4166, 4174)

Boat 4. Started breaking up . . . stern went up in air. After part briefly rights self. (Scott, Br 5673-5681)

Boat 4. "Very near." Suddenly sees *Titanic* sinking rapidly. Takes a plunge toward the bow, then two forward funnels seem to lean, then she seems to break in half as if cut with a knife, and as bow goes under, the lights go out. Stern stands up for several minutes, and then that, too, plunges down. (Ryerson, US 1108)

Boat 5. "She broke forward, and the after part righted itself and made another plunge and went right down." (Olliver, US 530-531)

Boat 5. No breaking up—went straight down. (Pitman, US 280; Br 15078-81)

Boat 5. Ship rises as though about to take a violent dive, then settles back; then stern rises, and down she goes. (Etches, US 818)

Boat 6. Went down intact, did not break up. (Peuchen, US 339)

Boat 10. Broke in two between third and fourth funnel. Stern section falls back horizontal, then tips and plunges. (Evans, US 753)

Boat 10. "She went down as far as the after funnel, and then there was a little roar, as though the engines had rushed forward, and she snapped in two, and the bow part went down and the after part came up and stayed up five minutes before it went down." (Buley, US 609-610)

Boat 12. Broke at first funnel. After part then righted itself after first part disappeared. (Poingdestre, Br 3108, 3111, 3117)

Boat 14. She almost stood up perpendicular . . . and presently she broke clean in two, probably two-thirds the length of the ship. After third—beyond after funnel—settled back, still floating. Then an explosion, and the after part turned on end and sank. (Crowe, US 620)

Collapsible A. Seemed as if the bow had broken off. (Brown, Br 10553, 10557)

Collapsible B. Bow was in the water, stern up. Then she exploded, throwing stern up out of the water. Stern floats for at least a minute, lights out. Then, "she turned over again and down she went." (Collins, US 630-631)

Collapsible B. Ship did not break in two. (Lightoller, Br 14075; US 69)

Collapsible B. Near perpendicular, then simply glided away. (Joughin, Br 6251-6266)

Collapsible D. Broke in two, after part briefly righted itself, then down. (Bright, US 839, 841)

Standing on poop. Gave a plunge and righted herself again. Then, as starts down again, after funnel seems to cant up and fall aft toward well deck. (Dillon, Br 3858-3869, 3883-3885)

Acknowledgments
and
Selected Sources

They are nearly all gone now. Of the 60-plus *Titanic* survivors who contributed so much to *A Night to Remember,* only a handful remain. Happily, Eva Hart still serves the best tea in Chadwell Heath; while across the Atlantic, Frank Acks is as chipper as ever in Norfolk, Virginia.

Gone, too, are most of the survivors I was never lucky enough to find 30 years ago, but who have since been such a pleasure to meet—for instance, Ruth Blanchard of Santa Barbara, California, and Marshall Drew of Westerly, Rhode Island.

Despite the erosions of time, there is still no lack of helpful people with fresh information on the *Titanic.* In some cases the families of survivors have come forward with letters and accounts retrieved from long-forgotten files. R. de Roussy de Sales has made available a fascinating letter from his uncle George Rheims that throws much light on the final minutes of the lost ship. Mary C. Barker has supplied a richly detailed manuscript by her vivacious grandmother, Helen Churchill Candee. Sally Behr Pettit has made available two accounts by her father, Karl Behr. Robert Maguire was no relative of Laura Mabel Francatelli, but he kindly sent me from his collection a typescript of a 19-page letter written by Miss Francatelli shortly after the *Carpathia*'s arrival in New York. Austin M. Fox has generously shared his extensive knowledge of Edward A. Kent, the Buffalo architect who went down with the ship.

Some of my most fruitful sources had no direct connection with the *Titanic* at all, but through the years have accumulated a great deal of information which they have placed at my disposal. A special salute goes to Rustie Brown, Edward de Groot, Roland Hauser, Ken Marschal, Alasdair McCrimmon, Patrick Stenson, and Tim Trower.

The dedicated officers of the *Titanic* Historical Society rate a paragraph of their own: Charlie Haas, President; Ed Kamuda, Secertary; and Jack Eaton, the Society's Historian. Even the lowliest stoker seems to have a welcome place in Mr. Eaton's archives.

Other persons have been helpful on specific aspects of the story. Their specialized knowledge, together with the written material I've been able to gather, form the backbone of my own research. The late David Watson, for instance, provided a penciled journal that gives a vivid picture of Harland & Wolff at the time the *Titanic* was built. He clearly felt the ship's plating was too thin.

But for flaws in the *Titanic*'s design, I depended most of all on J. Bernard Walker's *An Unsinkable Titanic* (Dodd, Mead, 1912). The actual building of the ship is covered in the "Special Number" of the magazine *Shipbuilder*, midsummer 1911 (reprint, Patrick Stephens, Ltd., 1983). The launching is described in the contemporary Belfast press and in "The Story of Harland & Wolff" by George Lavery and Alan Hedgley in the Fall 1980 issue of the *Titanic Commutator*, the lively quarterly of the *Titanic* Historical Society.

On Captain Smith's qualifications, I've benefited greatly from long discussions with marine historian John Maxtone-Graham, especially with regard to the *Olympic-Hawke* collision and the *Titanic*'s near-collision with the liner *New York*. For details on the *Olympic*'s encounter with the tug *O. L. Hallenbeck,* I'm indebted to Thomas Thacher, who retrieved the court record from some long-buried file in Hoboken, New Jersey. The superficial nature of the *Titanic*'s trials is clear from testimony at the British Inquiry.

For details on the *Titanic*'s maiden voyage up to the moment of collision, I'm grateful to various relatives and friends of survivors already mentioned. On the activities of "our coterie," I have also depended on Mrs. Candee's haunting account in the May 4, 1912, issue of *Collier's* magazine. The gamblers on board formed a world of their own, and it's fitting that they have an affectionate chronicler who has devoted himself to the subject. See George M. Behe's two-part article, "Fate Deals a Hand," in the *Commutator,* Fall and Winter, 1982.

There is no one left to interview on how the bridge handled the various wireless warnings of ice, but the testimony at the hearings gives a depressing picture of extreme casualness. Some mystery has surrounded the warning allegedly flashed by signal lamp from the steamer *Rappahannock* that last night. No one on the *Titanic* ever mentioned such an incident. The mystery is apparently cleared up by a story in *The New York Times* on April 27, 1912. It all happened on the 13th, not the 14th of April.

On the actual collision and First Officer Murdoch's last-second attempt to avoid it, I benefited greatly from a discussion with Fred M. Walker, Curator of Naval Architecture and Shipbuilding at the National Maritime Museum in England. On the damage suffered by the *Titanic* and the subsequent flooding of the vessel, I'm especially grateful to Alasdair McCrimmon of Toronto, Canada. I'm convinced that no member of the *Titanic*'s "black gang" knew his way around the bowels of the ship better than Mr. McCrimmon does today.

The shortage of lifeboats was an integral part of the tragedy. Recently it served as the basis for a major television documentary, *Titanic—a Question of Murder*, produced by Peter Williams. While I feel that the evidence does not support Mr. Williams's conclusions, I have the highest admiration for his generosity in putting me in touch with his sources, letting me draw my own conclusions. He has set a perfect example of professional courtesy.

In this connection, a special word of thanks to Dr. Alan Scarth of the Merseyside Maritime Museum in Liverpool for the sharp reproduction of a plan uncovered by Mr. Williams proposing 16 additional lifeboats. Unfortuately, the plan is not dated, nor is there any clue as to how hard the idea was pushed.

In piecing together the story of the Frederick Goodwin

family, I received generous assistance from the Reverend David Shacklock of Fulham, London. Additional information came from the contemporary press of Niagara Falls, New York. There's some confusion over the exact names and ages of various members of the family. I've depended on the Board of Trade files at the Public Record Office in London.

The *Titanic*'s band continues to intrigue students of the disaster, and I'm especially grateful to the hymnologists who I feel have set me straight on at least one part of the story. They include Roland Hind, Jessica M. Kerr, Merrill Knapp, and David Shacklock. The most helpful information of all came from a series of letters I received from Fred G. Vallance in 1957. Mr. Vallance was leader of the band on the Cunarder *Laconia* at the time of the disaster. He knew several of the *Titanic*'s musicians personally and, more than anyone else, he knew what they were likely to play under the circumstances. Colonel Gracie's remarks on how long the band played were contained in a lecture he gave at the University Club in Washington. Strangely, he left this information out of his well-known *The Truth About the Titanic*.

The troubles suffered by the bandsmen's families after the disaster run through the magazine *Musicians' Report and Journal* for much of 1912. I'm grateful to the Musicians' Union for the use of their file of this magazine. Finally, I'm indebted to Patrick Stenson for tapping some memories regarding the agents who represented the ships' musicians during this period.

On the *Californian*, I've benefited greatly from an interview and correspondence with the late Captain Charles Victor Groves, then Third Officer of that ship; from correspondence with Sir Ivan Thompson, former

Commodore of the Cunard Line, who personally knew several of those involved; from interviews with Jac Weller, a recognized expert witness on ballistics; and from a long, interesting letter from A. Brian Mainwaring, who served as a navigating officer with the White Star Line during the 1920's, and who also knew some of the individuals involved. I have also learned much from an engrossing manuscript written by Leslie Reade, who has devoted years to researching the *Californian*. If an unpublished book can be a *tour de force*, this is it.

The letter from Gerard J. G. Jensen to the President of the Board of Trade, which really opened up the *Californian* affair, can be found in the six boxes of Board of Trade material on the disaster at the Public Record Office in London (see MT 9/920, Item No. M12148). For Captain Lord's letter conceding "a certain amount of slackness" on the ship, see same file, Item No. M31921.

But as valuable as all these sources are, the most important evidence of all is readily accessible to anybody: It is the testimony given at the British Inquiry by the five men on the *Californian*'s bridge that night.

The defenders of the *Californian* are entitled to their say, too. They have written bushels on the subject. A selection of their work might include Peter Padfield's *The Titanic and the Californian* (Hodder and Stoughton, 1965); John C. Carrother's "Lord of the *Californian*," *United States Naval Institute Proceedings*, March 1968; Leslie Harrison's "The *Californian* Incident," *Merchant Navy Journal*, March 1962; petitions to the Board of Trade filed by the Mercantile Marine Service Association in Februry 1965 and in March 1968; and finally, almost any article on the ship in the *Titanic Commutator*.

Not surprisingly, the legal joustings over the *Titanic*

went on for years. I'm grateful to the present Lord Mersey for giving me the opportunity to spend a day at Bignor Park examining his great-grandfather's *Titanic* file. For background on the U.S. Senate's investigation, I depended mainly on Wyn Craig Wade's fine book *The Titanic: the End of a Dream* (Rawson Wade, 1979). The claims of passengers were well covered by *The New York Times* throughout 1912–1913; and the legal decisions, as the case wound its way through the courts, are all summarized by the Supreme Court in *Oceanic Steam Navigation Company* v. *Mellor*, 233 US 718. The parallel British case is *Ryan* v. *Oceanic Steam Navigation Company*, 3 K.B. 731, affirmed by the Court of Appeals, February 9, 1914. For guiding me through the whole labyrinth of "limited liability," I'm indebted to Eliot Lumbard, who is not only a member of the bar but a former third mate of the liner *Oriente*.

Details on the later years of various *Titanic* survivors come from a variety of sources, including personal friendships. Bruce Ismay's troubled life is described in numerous obituaries and in Wilton J. Oldham's *The Ismay Line* (Journal of Commerce, 1961). The Ben Hecht poem originally appeared in the *Chicago Daily Journal*, April 17, 1912. Craganour's disqualification is thoroughly explored in Sidney Galtrey's *Memoirs of a Racing Journalist* (Hutchinson, 1934). The Carter divorce was fully aired in the Philadelphia press. William T. Sloper's ordeal is covered in Sloper's privately published biography of his father, reprinted in the Spring 1984 issue of *Ship to Shore*, the magazine of the Oceanic Navigation Research Society.

The Duff-Gordons are covered by a good roundup

that appeared in the *New York Sunday News,* April 15, 1934. Details on confidence man George Brayton's return to business-as-usual were provided by survivor Edith Russell, who was falsely accused of complicity. The White Star Line's treatment of the *Titanic*'s surviving officers is touched on in Geoffrey Marcus's *Maiden Voyage,* paperback edition (Woodhill Press, 1977); and Commander Lightoller's heroism at Dunkirk is described in Patrick Stenson's *The Odyssey of C. H. Lightoller* (Norton, 1984).

The discovery of the *Titanic* was one of the major news stories of 1985. I'm grateful to Cathy Offinger (then Scheer), who was a navigator on the expedition, for clarifying many points that have puzzled me. For written accounts of the discovery, I've depended mainly on *The National Geographic,* December 1985; *Oceanus* magazine, Winter 1985; and the *Titanic Commutator,* Fall 1985. The *Knorr*'s brief side trip to photograph the submarine *Scorpion* is related in the September 23, 1985, issue of the *Navy Times.*

Throughout my research, the librarians, as always, stood ready to help. A special bow to the Earl W. Brydges Public Library of Niagara Falls, New York; the New York Society Library; the Newberry Library of Chicago; the Southhampton Public Libraries; and the Temple University Library.

In studying the *Titanic,* there's so much to explore that it sometimes seems there is no time left to write about it. Happily, I've had help from a small band of faithful researchers, including Preston Brooks, Evelyn Guss, Tom Longstreth, and (in London) Caroline Larken. Other helpful people pitched in on spot assignments: Elizabeth Hawn, Bob Meech, Steve Randolph, and Evan Thomas III come especially to mind.

Still others have added their professional expertise. Paul Pugliese provided the excellent map and chart. Colin Dawkins helped pull together the illustration section. Dr. Gerry Tidy photographed Mrs. Candee's miniature of her mother. I'm grateful to them all.

Finally, special thanks go to two pillars of strength who have been with the project from the start: my editor, Howard Cady, and the ever-patient Dorothy Hefferline, who prepared the manuscript and handled all correspondence. Unlike the *Titanic,* they really are unsinkable.

All the people mentioned in these Acknowledgments get much of the credit for any new light this book may throw on the *Titanic;* while the mistakes and shortcomings are all mine. As I pointed out 31 years ago in *A Night to Remember,* it is a rash man indeed who would set himself up as final arbiter on everything that happened the incredible night the *Titanic* went down.

Index

Wireless (*cont.*)
  procedures, 62–63, 71
  scenes in wireless shack,
    68–69
  24-hour watch, 17, 203
  see also Warning of ice
    ahead
"Women and children first,"
  93, 96
  interpretation port side, 116,
    152, 202
  interpretation starboard side,
    116, 122, 202, 217

Woolley, Douglas, 229–231
Woolner, Hugh, 51, 52, 54, 56,
  117, 118–119, 124, 128,
  223
Workmen's Compensation Act,
  146
Wright, Fred, 52

Y
Yates, Jay, 48

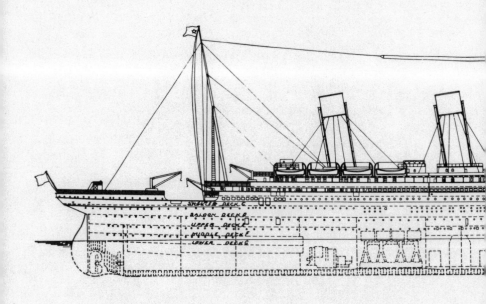

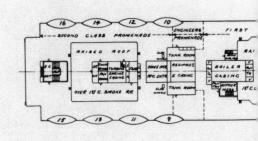

SHELTER DECK

SALOON DECK D

UPPER DECK E

MIDDLE DECK F

LOWER DECK G

16   14   12   10

----SECOND CLASS PROMENADE----   ENGINEERS
                                  PROMENADE   FIRST

                    RAISED ROOF   TANK ROOM   BOILER
                                    DOWN STR   RECIPROS   CASING   RAI
                              TURBINE FAN RFG. ENTR   E CASING
                              ENGINE   OFFICER
                              CASING   TANK ROOM   MESS   1ST CL

        OVER 1ST C. SMOKE RE   C

    15   13   11   9

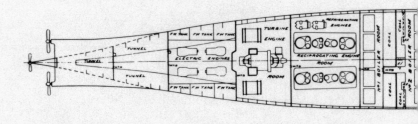

TUNNEL

TUNNEL   FW TANK FW TANK FW TANK   TURBINE   REFRIGERATING
                                                      ENGINE   ENGINES

TUNNEL   ----TUNNEL----   ELECTRIC ENGINES   COAL COAL No.1 BOILER ROOM
                                                              RECIPROCATING ENGINE   No.2 BOILER ROOM
                                                      WTD   ROOM   WTD   WTD
TUNNEL   FW TANK FW TANK FW TANK   ENGINE   COAL COAL